AF480869

IDEAL PARENTHOOD

THE JOURNEY FROM MOTHER'S WOMB UNTILL DEATH

DEVAANSHI WADI

Made with ♥ on the Notion Press Platform

www.notionpress.com

Marketed by-GyanambaVentures.pvt.ltd

Email id-gvpl70@gmail.com

CONTENTS

Contents

PART 2: PARENTING EARLY-CHILDHOOD   120

Contents

Acknowledgments

I extend my deepest gratitude to my parents, whose selfless decision and unwavering dedication shaped my journey. On my first birthday, they made a profound choice- to prioritize good parenting over a comfortable life in Mumbai. Though they had built a perfect life there, they believed that raising children in an environment rooted in discipline, values, ethics, and education was far more important. With that vision, we moved to Gulbarga, a smaller city with fewer luxuries but a space where strong moral foundation could be nutured. My childhood was more like rigorous training- structured, disciplined, and value driven- much like an Army upbringing. Looking back, I am deeply thankful for every lesson they instilled in me, for it has shaped me who I am today. I also extend my gratitude to all the great personalities who have inspired me to think beyond the ordinary, igniting my passion for growth and learning. Their wisdom has guided me on this path, and for that, I am forever grateful. Beyond this, I am immensely grateful for my spiritual journey, which has been a guiding force in my life. It has given me clarity, strength and a deeper understanding of my purpose. This path has been illuminated by the wisdom of great thinkers, mentors and experiences that have profoundly transformed my perspective. To all those who have inspired me to think beyond the ordinary and embrace spiritual growth, I offer my heartfelt thanks. Lastly, I extend my sincere appreciation to my publisher for believing in my vision and helping bring this book to life. With gratitude

Devaanshi wadi

Introduction

Parenting is one of the most profound responsibilities in life. It shapes not only an individual but also the very foundation of families, societies, and nations. The way a child is raised determines the kind of person they will become- whether they grow into individuals who contribute positively to the world or struggle to find their path. This book is a reflection of my journey, observations, and learnings about parenting and personal development. Growing up in an environment rooted in discipline, values and ethics. I experienced first hand the impact of conscious parenting. My parents made a bold decision to leave behind a comfortable life in Mumbai to ensure that I and my sibling were raised in an environment that prioritized character over convenience. Their choices, sacrifices, and vision have been the foundation of my understanding of ideal parenting.

As I progressed in life, my exposure to great personalities and my spiritual journey further deepened my perspective. I realized that parenting is not just about providing education and discipline; it is about shaping a child's mind, emotions, and soul. It is about nurturing them to become individuals who can bring positive changes to the world.

Beyond personal experiences and philosophical insights, this book also integrates scientific research and evidence-based findings to provide a well-rounded approach to parenting. By referring to studies in psychology, neuroscience, and child development. I aim to bridge the gap between traditional wisdom and modern science. Understanding how a child's brain develops, the impact of early experiences, and the role of emotional intelligence allows parents to make informed decisions that positively shape their children's future.

Through this book, I aim to share the principles and philosophies that I believe that contribute to ideal parenting. This is not just a guide for parents but a vision for creating a better world- one child at a time. If we wish to build a future filled with responsible, ethical, and strong individuals, it must begin at home.

I invite you to embark on this journey with me, to explore the deeper aspects of parenting, and to contribute to a world where the next generation is raised with wisdom, love and purpose.

HAPPY PARENTING!!!

PART 1

BEGINNING OF PARENTHOOD

PARENTING DURING PREGNANCY

Marriage: Beginning of Parenthood, Family and lifelong commitment

Marriage is more than a physical union, it is also a spiritual and emotional union, and this union mirrors the one between a flower and its fragrance.

Marriage is a bond like no other, it gives us a life partner, a team-mate, soul-mate as we move through the challenges of life together.

Marriage is designed for purity, when a marriage produces a child or adopts a child, it is one of life's greatest blessings. We may find around 40% of children being raised today are in a home with a single parent, and the effects of that facts are staggering (deeply shocking), In that Particular family, the father's absence leads to psychological disorders. This may lead to unethical issues.

But when children are brought up in a healthy marriage lifestyle, they get a front-row seat to see and experience the lasting benefits of strong a family.

An ideal marriage for ideal parenting is one where both parents create a supportive, balanced, and nurturing environment that allows both their relationship and family to flourish. In this kind of partnership, both parents are committed to their roles not only as spouses but also as co-parents, recognizing the relationship in shaping their children's well-being and development. Some important aspects for ideal marriage include-

Open communication- partners communicate openly and respectfully, addressing conflicts constructively. They work through differences and ensure a stable home atmosphere, helping children feel secure and teaching them positive communication skills.

Mutual respect and equality- both partners view each other as equals, sharing responsibilities, including emotional and practical care giving. This model of equality can help children learn about respect, fairness, and cooperation.

Emotional support and affection- showing genuine love and respect towards one another creates a warm, supportive home environment, reinforcing children's sense of security and the idea of healthy relationships.

Unified parenting approach- couples align on core parenting values and approaches, such as disciple, routines, and family values. Presenting a united front on important issues minimize confusion for children and creates consistency in the household.

Quality time together- balancing work, personal interests, and family time helps parents bond with each other and with their children. Engaging in shared activities fosters family unity and creates positive experiences that strengthen the parent-child relationship.

Role modeling- children learn a lot from observing their parent's interactions. An ideal marriage models healthy behaviors, such as patience, empathy, and compromise, showing children what respectfully relationships look like.

Emotional stability- parents prioritize self-care and mental well-being, understanding that their emotional health affects the family. Children benefit from emotionally stable parents who are able to respond thoughtfully rather than react impulsively.

Adaptability and resilience- life brings changes and challenges, and an ideal marriage for parenting needs adaptability and resilient behavior. This teaches children how to navigate difficulties with flexibility, togetherness, and optimism.

The goal isn't perfection but rather a nurturing, supportive relationship where both partners work together to create a strong foundation for their children.

"A STRONG MARRIAGE REQUIRES YOU TO LOVE EACH OTHER, ESPECIALLY WHEN YOU ARE STRUGGLING TO GEL WITH EACH OTHER."

"MARRIAGE IS LIKE A MUSIC BOTH ARE PLAYING DIFFERENT INSTRUMENTS & DIFFERENT PARTS BUT AS LONG AS YOU ARE PLAYING FROM THE SAME SHEET MUSIC, YOU CAN CREATE SOMETHING BEAUTIFUL.

Does Pregnancy need to be pre-planned?

Conceiving a child is not a part, but the process of parenting.

What's the difference between an unexpected guest & expected?

Yes, an unexpected guest surprises us with shock, fear and doubt. We won't be in a condition to welcome them and Justify "ATITHI DEVO BHAVA".

But on the other hand, the expected guest will be treated and welcomed with all the priorities.

Similarly expected child would be given all the priority, nurture and care. But an unexpected child would get all the benefits, but in a feeling of guilt, and surprise, finally, the feelings would be unstable and this leads to unstable parenting and personality development.

Pre-conception: Preparing for Parenthood

Preconception counseling helps you get ready for a healthy pregnancy. It's a good idea to meet with your doctor or midwife about three months before you start trying to have a baby. Even if you've been pregnant before, this checkup can help you plan better.

What happens during preconception counseling?

Your doctor will check many things about your health and your partner's health, including:

Your Medical History:

Tell your doctor about any health problems like diabetes, high blood pressure, epilepsy, or allergies.

Share details about any medicines you take, surgeries you've had, or issues in past pregnancies (like miscarriages).

Family Health History:

Let your doctor know if anyone in your family has health problems like diabetes, high blood pressure, birth defects, or other conditions.

Genetic Screening:

Some health problems, like sickle cell anemia or cystic fibrosis, can be passed from parents to children. Your doctor may recommend blood tests to check for these conditions.

Vaccinations:

Your doctor will make sure you're up to date on vaccines like rubella (German measles) and chickenpox. You need these vaccines before pregnancy because getting these diseases while pregnant can harm your baby.

Virus Exposure:

Let your doctor know if you've been exposed to viruses like Zika or COVID-19, as they can cause problems during pregnancy.

Intimate Partner Violence (IPV):

Your doctor might ask if you feel safe at home and in your relationships, as abuse can affect pregnancy.

Tests You Might Need

Your doctor might do these tests to check your health before pregnancy:

Blood Tests: To check your blood type and test for infections.

Pelvic Exam: To check the health of your reproductive organs (like the uterus and ovaries).

Pap Smear: To check for cancer in the cervix.

Physical Exam: To check your weight, blood pressure, and overall health.

This checkup helps find and fix any health issues early, so you can have a healthy pregnancy and baby.

How to Prepare Your Body for Pregnancy?

Follow these tips to improve your health before getting pregnant:

Avoid Alcohol:

Drinking alcohol can harm your fertility and affect your baby's health.

Alcohol during pregnancy can lead to serious problems like premature birth and developmental disorders.

Eat a Healthy Diet:

Choose fruits, vegetables, whole grains, lean proteins, and low-fat dairy.

Avoid processed, fatty foods and limit caffeine to 1–2 cups of coffee per day.

Avoid Harmful Substances:

Stay away from toxic chemicals, pesticides, and radiation (like X-rays). These can harm your baby's development.

Exercise and Maintain a Healthy Weight:

Regular exercise and a healthy weight reduce the risk of problems like high blood pressure or diabetes.

Being underweight can lead to low birth weight in babies.

Address Domestic Violence:

If you're in an abusive relationship, talk to your doctor or midwife for help and support.

Quit Smoking:

Smoking increases the risk of premature birth, low birth weight, and sudden infant death syndrome (SIDS).

Avoid second-hand and third hand smoke (smoke residue on clothing or furniture).

Reduce Infection Risks:

Avoid raw or undercooked meat, raw eggs, and cat litter to prevent harmful infections.

Wash your hands often and avoid sick people.

Take Vitamins:

Start taking a prenatal vitamin with 400 micrograms of folic acid.

Folic acid helps prevent birth defects in the baby's brain and spine.

These steps can help you and your baby stay healthy during pregnancy!

Beej sanskaar- An age old concept

Ayurveda offers a holistic approach to prepare couples for parenthood. This ancient practice focuses on cleansing and strengthening the body to ensure the best health for both parents and their future child.

Key Principles:

Cleansing and Renewal:

Ayurveda helps remove toxins, improve metabolism, strengthen immunity, and regulate digestion.

This creates a healthier body, ready to handle stress and fight diseases naturally.

Importance of Both Partners:

Ayurveda emphasizes preparing both the husband and wife before conception.

This preparation is seen as a preventative step that ensures lifelong benefits for the child.

Beej Sanskar:

What It Means: Beej sanskar involves preparing the "seeds" (sperm and ovum) to be pure and healthy.

Benefits: It helps create children who are strong, intelligent, and spiritually rich.

Positive Lifestyle Changes: Encourages parents to adopt healthier habits and emotional balance.

Deeper Connection: Strengthens the bond between parents and their future child by focusing on mindful and spiritual preparation.

Modern Integration:

Beej sanskar is now offered as classes, making it easier for couples to incorporate this tradition into their parenthood journey.

Why Choose Ayurveda?

This approach provides a strong foundation for conception and childbirth, blending traditional wisdom with modern health practices. By focusing on the health of both parents, Ayurveda aims to create a future generation that is healthy in body, mind, and spirit.

Infertility

What is Infertility?

Infertility is a condition where a person or couple is unable to conceive after trying for a specific period:

Under 35 years old: Diagnosed after 1 year of regular, unprotected sex.

35 years or older: Diagnosed after 6 months of regular, unprotected sex.

Pregnancy involves several steps: hormone production, egg release, sperm travel, fertilization, and embryo implantation. If any step is disrupted, pregnancy cannot occur.

Types of Infertility:

Primary Infertility: Never been pregnant before.

Secondary Infertility: Unable to conceive again after a previous pregnancy.

Unexplained Infertility: No identifiable cause.

Causes and Risk Factors

Common Risk Factors for Infertility:

Age (women over 35; men over 50).

Smoking, alcohol, and substance use.

Obesity or being underweight.

Chronic illnesses (e.g., diabetes, thyroid disease).

STIs or exposure to toxins (chemicals, radiation).

Female-Specific Causes:

Conditions like PCOS, endometriosis, or uterine fibroids.

Hormonal imbalances or poor egg quality.

Blocked fallopian tubes or structural issues.

Male-Specific Causes:

Low sperm count, poor sperm motility, or abnormal sperm shape.

Hormonal disorders, testicular injuries, or genetic conditions.

Exposure to high heat (tight clothing, hot tubs, carrying mobile phones, using laptops) or anabolic steroids.

Diagnosis of Infertility

Tests for Women:

Pelvic Exam: Check for structural issues.

Blood Tests: Measure hormone levels and ovulation.

Ultrasound & Hysteroscopy: Detect uterine or fallopian tube problems.

HSG Tests: Check for tubal blockages.

Tests for Men:

Semen Analysis: Evaluate sperm count and quality.

Blood Tests: Check hormones or genetic conditions.

Scrotal Ultrasound: Identify testicular problems like varicocele.

Treatment Options

Lifestyle Changes:

Stop smoking, drinking, or drug use.

Maintain a healthy weight and balanced diet.

Manage stress and time intercourse around ovulation.

Medical Treatments:

For Women: Fertility medications, surgeries (e.g., to open blocked tubes or remove fibroids).

For Men: Hormone therapy, surgeries (e.g., varicocele repair).

Assisted Reproductive Technology (ART):

In Vitro Fertilization (IVF): Fertilize eggs in a lab and transfer embryos to the uterus.

Intracytoplasmic Sperm Injection (ICSI): Inject a single sperm into an egg.

Intrauterine Insemination (IUI): Place sperm directly into the uterus.

Third-Party ART: Use donor eggs, sperm, embryos, or surrogates.

Unexplained Infertility

When no cause is found, treatments are based on test results and your healthcare provider's experience. Common approaches include:

ART, medications, and lifestyle adjustments.

Monitoring ovulation to improve timing of intercourse.

If you're struggling with infertility, consider seeking a second opinion or discussing aggressive treatment options with your provider. Patience and persistence can make a difference.

Miscarriage : spontaneous abortion

What is a Miscarriage?

A miscarriage is when a pregnancy ends unexpectedly before 20 weeks. Most miscarriages happen because the baby stops growing, and it's usually not something you caused.

Types of Miscarriages

Missed Miscarriage: The baby has stopped growing, but you don't have symptoms.

Complete Miscarriage: All pregnancy tissue has left the uterus.

Recurrent Miscarriage: When you've had three or more miscarriages in a row.

Threatened Miscarriage: You have bleeding or cramps, but the pregnancy might continue.

Inevitable Miscarriage: Bleeding and cramping happen, and the cervix opens, meaning a miscarriage is likely.

Signs of a Miscarriage

Heavy bleeding or passing clots/tissue.

Strong cramps or pain in the belly.

Back pain.

If you notice these symptoms, contact your doctor immediately.

Common Causes

Chromosome issues: The baby's genes didn't develop properly (happens by chance).

Other causes: Infections, hormone problems, uterine issues, smoking, drinking, or certain health conditions like diabetes or thyroid disease.

Diagnosis

Doctors use these tests to confirm a miscarriage:

Ultrasound: To check for the baby's heartbeat.

Blood tests: To check pregnancy hormone levels.

Pelvic exam: To see if the cervix has opened.

What Happens After a Miscarriage?

If all pregnancy tissue has left your body naturally, no treatment is needed. If not, your doctor may recommend:

Medication: Helps your body pass the tissue.

Surgery (D&C or D&E): Removes tissue safely.

Recovering After a Miscarriage

Expect light bleeding and mild cramps for a few days.

Avoid tampons, sex, or inserting anything into the vagina for at least two weeks.

See your doctor if you have heavy bleeding, fever, or severe pain.

Testing After Multiple Miscarriages

If you've had three or more miscarriages, doctors may recommend:

Genetic tests: For you, your partner, or the pregnancy tissue.

Blood tests: To check for hormone or immune problems.

Uterus checks: Using imaging or a small camera.

Can Miscarriages Be Prevented?

Most miscarriages can't be prevented, but taking care of yourself may help:

Go to all prenatal appointments.

Eat healthy and exercise regularly.

Avoid smoking, alcohol, and drugs.

Take prenatal vitamins.

Miscarriages are common and often not your fault. If you're concerned or have experienced one, reach out to your doctor for guidance and support.

Emotional aspects of Pregnancy:

How do emotions play a vital role in parenthood?

Emotional health is a vital aspect of overall well-being. When you feel calm and composed, it becomes easier to handle stress, maintain healthy relationships, and enjoy a fulfilling life. Taking care of your emotional health benefits not only you but also your baby, as it creates a nurturing environment for development.

Engaging in activities that promote a sense of purpose and belonging can enhance emotional well-being. Staying active, connected, and mindful of your mental state helps you face life's challenges with greater resilience.

During pregnancy, your baby is affected by various aspects of your daily life, including environmental sounds, the air you breathe, the food you consume, and, importantly, your emotions. Maintaining a positive and calm state allows your baby to grow in a supportive environment. On the other hand, feelings of stress and anxiety can increase certain hormones in your body, which may influence your baby's brain and body development.

The interactions between you and your baby, even before birth, help shape their emotional, cognitive, and social development. These early connections lay the foundation for the emotional bonds you'll share with your child throughout life.

What If I'm Struggling with My Emotions?

It's common for one or both parents to face emotional challenges during pregnancy or after a baby's arrival. It's important to understand that these feelings are normal, and you are not alone. Parenthood often brings a mix of emotions—joy, love, worry, exhaustion, and sometimes guilt or frustration. These feelings can feel overwhelming, but they are a natural part of the journey.

Here are some tips that may help:

Acknowledge Your Emotions: Recognize and accept your feelings without judgment. Experiencing negative emotions doesn't make you a bad parent—it's simply part of adjusting to a new phase in life.

Take Small Breaks: Even short moments to yourself, like a walk or enjoying a cup of tea, can help you recharge.

Connect with Others: Sharing your experiences with other parents, friends, or family members can be comforting. You might also find support through a partner or a professional who can listen without judgment.

Practice Self-Compassion: Be gentle with yourself. Remind yourself that parenting doesn't have to be perfect—doing your best is more than enough.

Adjust Expectations: Let go of rigid ideas about how things "should" be. Focus on being a "good enough" parent, allowing space for learning and growth.

If these feelings persist or feel overwhelming, reaching out to a counselor or therapist can provide tailored support. Parenthood is a shared experience, and there are many resources available to help you navigate this time. You are never alone in this journey, and with patience and support, you can find your way through.

Becoming a mother?

Motherhood is a process that can start prior to conception when a woman decides or has the desire to become pregnant. Ultimately being a mother, means a lot, your hopes and dreams have come true. You may love feeling your baby move inside. you may feel a sense of achievement in giving birth. It is a feeling that can't be expressed in words but, can be felt.

Motherhood is the experience of being a mother, with all the roles, responsibilities, emotions, and changes it brings. It often involves nurturing and caring a child, guiding them through life's stages, creating a sense of security and love. Beyond biology, motherhood is about the unique bond that develops between a caregiver and a child.

Motherhood is a dynamic journey, often marked by selflessness, beyond personal growth, and moments of joy and challenge. Many describe it as transformative, as it changes one's identity, priorities, and perspective on life. The experience can be deeply rewarding yet demanding, bringing with immense personal growth as well as moments of uncertainty.

You may love holding, touching watching, smelling and playing with your baby. Few mothers may not feel this in the initial stage, not an issue; you can start bonding with your baby by focusing on it.

Sometimes the happy emotions of motherhood are mixed up with different feelings like loss, fear, worry, guilt and frustration, you might think; what if I make too many mistakes? Whether people will think that I'm a bad mother? What about my previous life?

It is normal to ask yourself a lot of questions when you are going through a major life change like having a baby. So, clarify all your doubts and then accept motherhood.

Becoming a mother is an ongoing journey of learning and growth. While it may come with challenges, it also brings a deep sense of fulfillment and purpose. Motherhood is as much about growing as a person as it is about raising a child. It's an experience that evolves over time, and the love and bond between a mother and her child often last a lifetime.

Becoming a mother by choice and without choice makes a lot of difference, so motherhood should be your utmost priority for a successful parenting. Remember just by giving birth one can't be a parent; it's an emotion, which makes you equal to the almighty god.

Becoming a father?

While women usually start preparing emotionally for parenthood during pregnancy, some fathers may understand at a later stage. As a result, the reality of fatherhood could be a shock. Even if you have been preparing throughout the pregnancy, some fathers might not be prepared for the reality of having a newborn baby.

Some fathers can feel fierce, overprotective, overwhelming love towards their children straight away, for others it may take a bit longer. Fatherhood is just as challenging as motherhood, though not always for the same reasons.

You might think I want to help with the baby, but I don't know how? Is it stressful managing work and family commitments?

You might also notice your relationship with your partner changes a lot too. It's normal to feel confused, stressed and out of your comfort zone when you have a new baby. With any new or difficult situation, sometimes you can cope with the challenge and sometimes you may not feel overwhelmed.

Becoming a father is a life-changing journey, filled with excitement, challenges, and deep emotions. It's natural to feel a mix of joy, fear, pride, and uncertainty as you prepare for this new role. Here are some thoughts to help you navigate this transition:

Acknowledge Your Feelings-It's okay to feel overwhelmed or unsure at times. Many new fathers worry about their ability to provide, protect, or connect with their child. Give yourself permission to feel everything—good or bad. It's all part of the process.

Build Your Confidence-Learn as much as you can: Reading, attending prenatal classes, or talking to other dads can help you feel more prepared.

Be present- Being there for your partner during pregnancy and birth builds your connection with your child and your confidence in your role.

Support Your Partner-Parenthood is a team effort. Supporting your partner emotionally and physically during pregnancy, birth, and beyond strengthens your bond and creates a positive foundation for your family.

Create a Bond-Spend time with your baby, even in the early days when they mostly sleep and cry. Things like holding, feeding, talking, or skin-to-skin contact help build your relationship.

Be patient—it's normal for bonding to take time, especially if this is your first child.

Take Care of Yourself-Adjusting to fatherhood can be exhausting. Make time to rest, eat well, and seek support when needed. Don't hesitate to talk about how you're feeling with a friend, family member, or counsellor. Men often feel pressure to suppress emotions, but expressing them can be a relief.

Focus on the Big Picture-Fatherhood isn't about being perfect; it's about showing up, being present, and learning along the way. Mistakes happen, but what matters is your commitment to your child's well-being and growth.

Parenthood is a journey, not a destination, and you'll learn so much as you go. Trust yourself, lean on your support network, and remember that your love and effort will make a lasting difference in your child's life.

Fatherhood is the experience of raising, guiding, and nurturing a child, typically as their father or a father figure. It's not just about biological ties but about the deep, lasting bond formed through care, love, and presence. Fatherhood encompasses a wide range of roles and responsibilities, and its meaning can evolve over time.

Fatherhood today is about more than just being the "breadwinner." Modern fathers are often deeply involved in care giving, emotional support, and day-to-day parenting tasks. It's about being actively present in their child's life and building a relationship based on trust, love, and respect.

Ultimately, fatherhood is a journey of personal growth as much as it is about raising a child. It challenges you to develop patience, empathy, and strength while fostering a sense of joy and fulfilment in watching your child grow and thrive.

Some Common Emotional Problems in Parents

Pregnancy and the postpartum period can bring various emotional challenges. These are often mistakenly grouped under "postnatal depression," which can be misleading, as emotional struggles can occur during pregnancy too.

Baby Blues

During the first week after giving birth, up to 80% of mothers may experience the "baby blues." This is a period of heightened sensitivity characterized by crying, irritability, anxiety, and mood swings. These feelings typically peak around 3 to 5 days postpartum and are largely due to hormonal changes. The symptoms usually resolve on their own within a few days with emotional support, understanding, and assistance in caring for the baby. However, if these feelings persist beyond two weeks, it could indicate the onset of postnatal depression.

Adjustment Challenges

Adjusting to the significant life changes brought on by a new baby is a common experience. For most, this adjustment phase is temporary and manageable. However, some individuals may find it more challenging, leading to ongoing distress. In such cases, family support and professional advice can be beneficial.

Attachment Difficulties

Many parents expect to feel an immediate bond with their baby, but for some, this connection may take days or weeks to develop. This can lead to feelings of guilt, stress, or disappointment. If there's a persistent lack of connection, parents may feel distant or even negatively toward the baby. With adequate rest and support, most parents begin to feel attached to their baby. If these feelings persist beyond a couple of weeks, seeking guidance from a trusted source is recommended.

Anxiety

A certain level of worry is natural, but excessive anxiety can interfere with daily life and parenting. Severe anxiety may manifest as fear of losing control, low self-confidence, or believing one is an inadequate parent. Research suggests that 14-16% of women experience clinical anxiety during pregnancy and 8-10% after childbirth. Symptoms can include panic attacks, restlessness, irritability, and excessive concern about the baby's safety. If these feelings become overwhelming, it's essential to seek help from a healthcare provider.

Depression

Approximately 8-11% of women experience depression during pregnancy, and about 13% experience it postpartum. Symptoms may include persistent sadness, feelings of failure or guilt, irritability, withdrawal from social contact, and, in severe cases, thoughts of self-harm or suicide. If these feelings persist or intensify, it's crucial to seek professional support. Immediate help is necessary if there are thoughts of harm to oneself or others.

Postpartum Psychosis

This rare but severe condition affects 1 or 2 in every 1,000 mothers and should not be confused with postnatal depression. Those with a personal or family history of bipolar disorder or schizophrenia are at higher risk. Symptoms may include confusion, delusions, hallucinations, intense emotional highs, and a reduced need for sleep. This condition requires urgent medical attention to ensure the safety of both mother and baby.

PHOBIAS: Emotional Health for New Parents

It's normal for parents-to-be to feel some fear or anxiety about having a baby. However, some individuals experience specific and intense fears or phobias related to pregnancy or childbirth, such as an extreme fear of giving birth (tokophobia) or fear of blood or needles.

A phobia is characterized by a persistent and exaggerated fear of a particular object or situation. People with phobias often recognize that their fear is disproportionate, but it can significantly impact their daily lives.

Tokophobia

While many expectant parents experience some level of apprehension about childbirth, tokophobia is a severe, pathological fear of giving birth. Women with tokophobia may feel overwhelmed, regret becoming pregnant, or even avoid pregnancy altogether. This fear can lead to feelings of being trapped, insecure, or inferior compared to others who seem more at ease with the process.

Blood and Needle Phobia

The fear of blood (hemophobia) or needles can cause a strong physical reaction, including a rapid increase in heart rate and blood pressure, followed by a sudden drop that may result in fainting. These fears can be particularly distressing during situations like blood tests, IV treatments, or seeing blood during or after childbirth.

If these fears or phobias interfere with your well-being or daily life, it's important to seek help. Speaking with a doctor, counsellor, or psychologist can provide strategies and support to manage these challenges effectively.

The relationship between you and your partner:

Pregnancy often brings significant changes to a relationship, especially if it's your first baby. While some couples adapt easily, others may find the transition more challenging. It's normal for occasional disagreements to arise during this time, but pregnancy can also be a time for deeper connection and understanding.

Here are some tips to help strengthen your relationship during pregnancy:

Communicate Openly

Share your feelings about the pregnancy, both positive and negative. Expressing your thoughts openly can foster understanding and closeness.

Focus on explaining your perspectives without placing blame.

Discuss your hopes and dreams for your growing family, including traditions and values that matter to each of you.

Talk about parenting styles and work together to address any differences, finding solutions through negotiation and mutual understanding.

Be honest about your sexual needs and any changes in intimacy during this time.

Practical Steps to Strengthen Your Bond

Attend antenatal classes together to prepare for the journey ahead as a team.

If financial concerns arise, consider seeking advice on budgeting for a baby to reduce stress.

Discuss how you'll make time for each other as a couple, even after the baby arrives.

Plan how to share household responsibilities now and after your baby is born to ensure balance and fairness.

If you find that these strategies aren't enough or if you're struggling with your relationship, don't hesitate to consult a doctor or counsellor for additional support. Pregnancy is a time of growth, and seeking help can ensure you navigate this journey together with confidence and care.

The relationship between you and your family and friends:

Managing Support and Advice during Pregnancy

Pregnancy is a special time not only for you and your partner but also for the people around you, such as family and friends, who may take a keen interest in your journey. Their support and enthusiasm can be invaluable, and their help may come in many forms. However, it's also common to feel overwhelmed if their involvement starts to feel intrusive or if you find yourself on the receiving end of excessive advice or even criticism.

While some advice may be helpful and appreciated, not all of it will suit your needs or preferences. The key is to focus on what feels right for you and your partner. After all, it's your baby, and the decisions about parenting and preparation ultimately belong to you.

If unsolicited advice becomes overwhelming, try addressing the situation gently. You might explain that while you value their concern, certain decisions are personal and best made by you and your partner. Setting these boundaries early can help create a balance between accepting support and maintaining your independence.

Remember, this is your journey, and it's okay to make choices that align with your values and priorities.

Coping if you are alone

Support during Pregnancy When You're On Your Own

Being pregnant on your own can feel challenging at times, but having a support system can make a big difference. Whether the challenges are personal or medical, it's important to reach out to someone you trust rather than trying to handle everything on your own.

Find someone who can provide emotional or practical support during this special time. This could be a close friend, sibling, or even your mother. Remember, you don't have to attend antenatal appointments or go through labour alone. You have the right to bring someone you trust with you to these events, and their presence can be reassuring.

If you don't have a partner, consider involving your chosen support person in antenatal classes. You can also ask your midwife if there are any antenatal classes specifically designed for single parents in your area.

As you prepare for the baby's arrival, think about how you'll manage after the birth. Identify people who might be able to help and support you during this time. If you feel isolated or don't have anyone nearby, reach out to a healthcare professional or local support groups for guidance and assistance.

Remember, you're not alone, and there are resources and people ready to support you through this journey.

For more information refer to single-parent, adoption chapters.

When a Relationship doesn't work –Relationship Breakdown and Divorce:

Coping with Relationship Breakdown

The end of a relationship can be a challenging and emotional time for everyone involved. Along with managing your own feelings, you might also worry about how to support your child through the transition. While separation or divorce can be difficult, there are steps you can take to help your family navigate this period.

If you're going through a separation, it's normal to experience a range of intense emotions, such as anger, fear, confusion, guilt, or rejection. These feelings can feel overwhelming, but it's important to remember that many people work through the complexities of separation and go on to lead fulfilling lives.

One key to moving forward is recognizing that you can be a successful and loving parent, no matter your family circumstances. Your ability to provide stability, care, and love for your child is what truly matters.

If you're finding it difficult to cope, don't hesitate to seek support. Speaking with a counsellor or therapist can provide valuable guidance and help you manage your emotions during this challenging time.

For more information refer single-parent chapter.

Treatment options for Parents experiencing Emotional problems:

Individual Counselling

This involves talking to a counsellor who provides a supportive, non-judgmental space to discuss your concerns. The goal is to help you work through personal challenges in a safe environment.

Individual Psychotherapy

Psychotherapy focuses on understanding the deeper issues that might make you vulnerable to mental health challenges like anxiety or depression. It helps address the root causes of these problems to promote long-term well-being.

Couple Counselling

This type of therapy is designed for couples, helping partners understand each other better and strengthen their relationship. Pregnancy and childbirth can put stress on relationships, and counselling can help manage these pressures and improve communication.

Support Groups

Led by health professionals like community nurses or social workers, support groups offer a space to share experiences, gain useful information, and develop practical skills. These groups provide emotional support and guidance from others in similar situations.

Practical Support at Home

This involves help with everyday tasks like cooking, cleaning, and caring for children, allowing you to adjust to life with your new baby. Support can come from family, friends, or well-wishers.

Medication

Medication can be an important part of managing mental health disorders, particularly when combined with therapy and other support services. Always take medication as prescribed by a healthcare professional to ensure proper dosage and timing.

Admission to Hospital

In cases of severe emotional distress, hospitalization may be necessary. This is especially important if there's a risk of harm to yourself or your baby. If you or your loved ones feel concerned about your safety, seeking professional help is crucial.

Lifestyle Changes and Alternative Treatments

Research shows that therapeutic lifestyle changes can significantly improve mental health. These changes are not only effective but also inexpensive and beneficial for physical health. They can complement other forms of treatment.

Exercise: Regular exercise has been shown to boost mood by increasing serotonin, dopamine, and endorphin levels. It can reduce stress and improve overall well-being. Before starting any exercise routine, consult your doctor to ensure it's safe for you.

Diet: A healthy diet is essential, particularly during pregnancy or after childbirth. Your body goes through significant nutritional demands during this time. A balanced diet supports both physical and emotional health.

Relaxation, Yoga, and Meditation: Relaxation techniques like progressive muscle relaxation, yoga, and meditation can help reduce stress, ease muscle tension, and improve emotional health. Yoga combines physical postures with breathing techniques, while meditation can be practiced alone or as part of a yoga class.

Alternative Medications: Herbal products are sometimes used for mild mental health issues, but they may not be safe during pregnancy or breastfeeding. Always consult your doctor before using any alternative treatments, as they may interact with other medications.

Computer or Internet Programs: Online programs provide structured activities and resources to help manage mental health issues. These can be a helpful tool in addition to other forms of support.

Sleep

Adequate sleep (at least 8 hours) is essential for emotional well-being. While getting enough rest can be difficult during pregnancy or after childbirth, try to prioritize sleep as much as possible.

Importance of Nutrition and Physical activity during Pregnancy

Importance of Nutrition during Pregnancy

Eating a balanced diet is one of the most important habits during pregnancy. Proper nutrition helps you meet the increased demands on your body as your pregnancy progresses. The goal is to consume enough nutrients to support your baby's growth and maintain a healthy weight for yourself.

Pregnancy typically requires about 300 extra calories per day. These calories should come from a well-rounded diet rich in proteins, fruits, vegetables, and whole grains. Sweets and fats should be kept to a minimum. A nutritious, balanced diet during pregnancy can also help alleviate common pregnancy symptoms such as nausea and constipation.

Research shows that factors like high body mass index (BMI) before pregnancy, excessive weight gain, and poor nutrition during pregnancy can increase the risk of non-communicable diseases (NCDs) and may negatively impact both the duration of pregnancy and the post-pregnancy period. Both underweight and overweight individuals face a higher risk of developing metabolic diseases later in life.

Unbalanced nutrition and micronutrient deficiencies during pregnancy can lead to under nutrition in both the mother and the unborn child. Nutrition encompasses factors such as BMI, body composition, and the foods consumed all of which impact whether the body receives the necessary nutrients. When there's an imbalance between the body's nutritional needs and actual intake before, during, and after pregnancy, it can influence the baby's early development, increasing the risk of obesity and chronic diseases later in life.

Studies suggest that the rise in obesity may be linked to inadequate prenatal nutrition, followed by poor dietary habits (high in fat, salt, and sugar) later in life.

The Effect of Maternal diet before and after Pregnancy on the Lifelong Health of the Child

Fetal development is highly dependent on the proper supply of nutrients, including micronutrients, in the mother's bloodstream. Maternal nutrition has a direct impact on the child's long-term health, and it plays a significant role in the global rise of obesity and non-communicable diseases. There is also a clear connection between low birth weight and an increased risk of various diseases in adulthood, such as insulin-related metabolic disorders, Type 2 diabetes, obesity, hypertension, heart disease, and kidney disorders.

Obesity before and after conception raises the risk of complications during pregnancy. It increases the likelihood of arterial hypertension (high blood pressure) and gestational diabetes (diabetes during pregnancy), which can have negative health consequences for both the mother and the child. Obesity is also the primary cause of macrosomia (excessive birth weight), which can affect the child's glucose and lipid metabolism and lead to hypertension.

Before and during pregnancy, women and their partners should be well-informed about the importance of a healthy lifestyle for the long-term health of both the mother and the child. Special attention and tailored dietary advice should be provided to pregnant women in the following situations:

Maternal Obesity: This condition is associated with a higher risk of miscarriage, premature birth, gestational diabetes, and hypertension for the mother, and a higher risk of obesity, heart disease, and neural tube defects for the baby.

Pregnancy After Gastrointestinal Surgery: Women who have had gastrointestinal procedures may be at risk for deficiencies in essential vitamins and minerals, leading to anaemia in the mother and complications for the child.

Adolescent Pregnancy: Teenage pregnancies are often linked to poor nutrition, alcohol consumption, and smoking, which pose health risks for both the mother and the child.

Substance Use: Pregnant women who use tobacco, alcohol, or drugs should seek professional help and guidance for both their health and the health of their baby.

Multiple Pregnancy: Multiple fetuses require careful monitoring to ensure that the nutritional needs of both the mother and babies are met.

Low Income: Pregnant women with limited financial resources may struggle to access a balanced, nutritious diet.

Special Diets: Pregnant women following vegan, fruitarian, or macrobiotic diets may face a higher risk of deficiencies in protein, vitamins, and minerals.

Gastrointestinal Disorders: Women with a history of gastrointestinal diseases may experience poor nutrient absorption.

Mental Health Conditions: Pregnant women with a history of mental health disorders should receive additional support to manage both their physical and emotional well-being.

Pregnant women with any of these conditions should receive personalized nutritional guidance from a dietician or nutritionist to ensure best for both their health and the health of their baby.

Does Nutrition has Effect on our Baby's Genes

Have you ever wondered why we look and behave similar to one of our parents while our siblings are copy of the other parent or sometimes both are same, why is it? because of our luck or there is a reason. The answer is science.

According to recent research the time of pregnancy, nutrition and seasons are interlinked. Let me breakdown it with my example, I have more similarities with my Father though it may be physical characters or my behaviour, but my brother is copy of my mother, now why so? Now by birth month is December as I am premature, the conception month(when I entered her womb) would be April, and now I have to compare it with my parents, my Father's conception month would be June, and my Mother's would be October. Now see whose conception month is more close to me, yes my Father. My brother' conception month is also October. Did you see something, yes the conception month has decided our genes.

But how, the answer is the seasonal food the mother had during pregnancy, which has triggered the similar genes. Now you also can calculate why you are similar to one of your parent, just check whose conception month is near to your conception month. Thus we can say how important nutrition is for development of our baby. It determines our baby's physical features, mental abilities, behaviour and character etc.

Nutrition During Pregnancy

Pregnant women require only a slight increase in energy intake during pregnancy. In the first trimester (the first three months), only an additional 100 kcal per day is needed, while in the second and third trimesters, the increase is around 300 kcal per day. Overall, pregnant women need about 10 to 15% more calories than before pregnancy, particularly during the final months. However, this additional energy can be obtained from a relatively small quantity of food. Many expectant mothers tend to overestimate their caloric needs, but the recommended increase depends on factors like basal metabolic rate, lifestyle, and physical activity.

Proteins

Protein is crucial during pregnancy as it is the primary building block for maternal and fetal tissues. Pregnant women should aim for 60 grams of protein daily. Insufficient protein intake can increase the risk of the child developing conditions like diabetes, heart disease, obesity, or high blood pressure later in life. Additionally, inadequate protein is associated with low birth weight.

Carbohydrates

Carbohydrates are the primary source of energy for both the mother and the child. Glucose from carbohydrates serves as the optimal fuel for brain function. During pregnancy, carbohydrates should make up 50 to 60% of total energy intake. The consumption of sugar should be limited to no more than 5% of total energy intake, as excess sugar can increase the risk of obesity. Expectant mothers should avoid sweetened soft drinks, which are also linked to an increased risk of pre-eclampsia and premature birth.

Fats

Fats are an essential part of the diet, providing energy and supporting various metabolic processes. Pregnant women do not need to increase their fat intake but should aim for fats to make up about 30% of total energy intake. Saturated fats, found in butter, cream, fatty meats, and palm oil, should be limited, and trans fats—often found in partially hydrogenated vegetable oils used in dairy and confectionery products—should be avoided.

Fibre

A diet rich in fibre is beneficial during pregnancy and lactation, promoting heart health, reducing the risk of diabetes, preventing constipation, and decreasing the risk of pre-eclampsia. Fibre also provides nutrient-dense, low-energy foods. The recommended fibre intake is around 30 to 35 grams per day. Fibre-rich foods also contain minerals, vitamins, and other biologically active substances.

Vitamins & Minerals

The requirements for vitamins and minerals during pregnancy are significantly higher than for additional energy intake. Expectant mothers should focus on the quality of the foods they consume to balance their diet. Most women require additional nutrients only after the fourth month of pregnancy. However, certain micronutrients, such as folic acid and iron, are crucial before conception and during early pregnancy.

Water

Pregnant women need 2 to 2.5 litres of liquid per day, primarily in the form of water. This requirement should increase gradually as the pregnancy progresses, especially as the woman gains weight. In the final month of pregnancy, an additional 300 ml of water per day may be needed. Adequate hydration supports vital functions and reduces the risk of urinary infections, kidney stones, and constipation.

Caffeine

Excessive caffeine intake can restrict fetal development. It is recommended that pregnant women consume no more than 200 mg of caffeine per day. Caffeine content varies in different foods and drinks; for example, two cups of coffee or four small mugs of tea contain approximately 200 mg of caffeine. Energy drinks containing caffeine should be avoided during pregnancy.

Alcohol

Alcohol consumption during pregnancy is harmful to the fetus. Children exposed to alcohol in utero may suffer from various physical and mental disorders, both before and after birth, and throughout their lives. These children may experience growth impairments and neural disorders, leading to serious learning and behavioural issues. Even smaller amounts of alcohol can lead to milder but similar symptoms. Research shows that consuming more than one alcoholic drink per day during pregnancy increases the risk of premature birth and low birth weight. Therefore, the safest approach is complete abstinence from alcohol during pregnancy and lactation.

Balanced Nutrition during Pregnancy

A comprehensive, balanced diet provides all the essential nutrients required by the body for growth, maintenance of health, and disease prevention. It includes a variety of recommended foods in quantities suited to each individual's weight, physical activity level, and any metabolic concerns.

Cereals

Among all cereals, whole grains should be prioritized. Whole grain products and potatoes are excellent sources of complex carbohydrates, vitamins, minerals, and fiber. However, it is important to avoid using excessive amounts of fats and oils when preparing these foods.

Vegetables and Fruits

Vegetables and fruits are crucial sources of vitamins, minerals, and antioxidants. It is recommended to consume two to four servings of fruit and four to five servings of vegetables per day. Vegetables should be fresh, and over-salted or deep-fried varieties should be avoided. Fresh fruits are preferable, while tinned fruits should be avoided. Fruit juices should be 100% fruit juice, as fruit drinks or nectars often contain added sugars, sweeteners, or other undesirable additives.

Dairy Products

Dairy products are vital sources of protein, calcium, and iodine. However, products high in fat or sugar, such as full-fat dairy and sugary yogurts, should be avoided. Preference should be given to unsweetened fermented dairy products like kefir, buttermilk, and natural yogurt. Cottage cheese is a good source of protein and calcium, while cheese-like products containing trans fats should be excluded from the diet.

Protein-containing Products

Lean meats and eggs are excellent sources of protein and iron. Meat should be stewed or roasted, but not overcooked. Processed products such as sausages and smoked meats should be avoided, as they contain less protein and higher amounts of salt, fat, and additives. Fish, especially oily fish, is an important source of omega-3 fatty acids and vitamin D. It is recommended to consume two servings of fish per week, one of which should be oily fish. Plant-based protein sources, such as legumes, nuts, and seeds, are also essential parts of a healthy diet.

Oils

Oils should provide sufficient amounts of monounsaturated fats or omega-3 fatty acids, which are beneficial for heart health and overall well-being.

Unhealthy and Dangerous substances in the diet during Pregnancy

Certain substances in food may have no nutritional value and can adversely affect the health of both the mother and the fetus. It's important to consult a doctor before incorporating them into the diet.

Artificial Sweeteners

There are various sweeteners, such as saccharin, acesulfame, and aspartame, that can cross the placental barrier and appear in breast milk. However, both sweeteners and sucralose have been found to be safe for mothers and fetuses. Aspartame should be avoided by women with Phenylketonuria (PKU), as it is metabolized into phenylalanine, which is toxic to the fetal brain. Stevia, a plant-based sweetener, appears to have no adverse effects on fetal development. It's advisable to minimize the use of artificial sweeteners and opt for natural alternatives.

Bisphenol A (BPA)

Bisphenol A is known to adversely affect the endocrine system and may disrupt hormone-dependent tissues in the fetus, such as thyroid function. It may also increase the risk of spontaneous abortion. BPA is found in polycarbonate plastics, also known as "hard plastics," and can migrate into food when it comes into contact with these materials. It's essential to choose BPA-free containers, and infant feeding bottles containing BPA have been banned in most countries. Always check the labels of containers to ensure they are free from BPA.

Polychlorinated Biphenyls (PCBs) and Dioxins

PCBs and dioxins are lipophilic substances that accumulate in fats, particularly in oily fish and fish liver. Pregnant women should limit their intake of these substances by avoiding consumption of fish more than once a week, especially fatty fish.

Lead

High levels of lead intake are linked to increased risks of hypertension and spontaneous abortion in the mother, as well as low birth weight and impaired neural development in the infant. Lead can be absorbed from low-quality enamel vessels, lead-containing glassware, or certain cookware, such as old Teflon-coated pans. It's advisable to avoid using such cookware and ensure that your dishes and utensils are lead-free.

Vitamin A

Pregnant women should avoid consuming liver or liver products, as well as supplements containing retinol, including fish oil. However, plant-based products containing carotenes, such as red and orange vegetables and fruits, are safe for consumption during pregnancy and do not pose a risk to the fetus.

Mercury

Mercury accumulates in large ocean fish such as shark, marlin, tuna, swordfish, and king mackerel. Pregnant women should avoid consuming these types of fish. Additionally, mercury can accumulate in larger freshwater fish, such as Northern Pike, and should be limited to no more than one serving per week. Consumption of tuna should not exceed 140g per week to minimize mercury exposure.

Safe Nutrition

Pregnancy causes partial suppression of the immune system, which increases the risk of foodborne infections. To minimize this risk, it is essential to adhere to strict hygiene practices when preparing food, ensuring adequate heat treatment of eggs, meat, and fish.

Toxoplasmosis

Toxoplasma gondii, a protozoan parasite, can be found in uncooked animal products, as well as in vegetables and berries contaminated with infected soil. Therefore:

Thoroughly wash all vegetables and fruits that may have come into contact with soil.

Avoid consuming meat that has not been adequately cooked or has undergone only light heat treatment, as Toxoplasma cysts can survive in frozen or smoked meat.

Listeriosis

Listeriosis is caused by the bacterium Listeria monocytogenes, which thrives in improperly stored food and can proliferate in the refrigerator. The bacteria can cross the placental barrier, potentially infecting the fetus. To prevent infection:

Avoid consuming raw, unpasteurized milk and its products.

Do not consume food past its expiration date and store food properly.

Avoid soft cheeses made from unpasteurized milk (e.g., brie, feta, blue cheese).

Be cautious with raw or undercooked animal products, including meat, fish, eggs, and seafood.

Salmonellosis and Other Infections

Uncooked or undercooked animal products, including raw meat, sausages, hams, uncooked fish, seafood, and eggs, pose a risk for infections such as Salmonellosis. To minimize risk:

Do not consume raw or undercooked animal products.

Avoid sprouted seeds, grains, and beans.

Thaw frozen meat in the refrigerator, not at room temperature.

General Hygiene and Storage Guidelines

Wash your hands thoroughly before handling food.

Use separate kitchen utensils for cooked and uncooked products.

Wash vegetables, salad leaves, and fruits carefully before consumption.

Store food grown in soil or close to the soil separately from other food.

Consume food immediately after cooking, and follow proper storage practices to prevent contamination.

By maintaining good hygiene practices and avoiding risky foods, you can help protect both yourself and your baby from foodborne illnesses during pregnancy.

Vitamins, Minerals & other Food Supplements

A balanced and healthy diet before conception and during pregnancy generally provides all the essential nutrients needed, with the exception of folic acid and iodine. A well-rounded diet offers a wide range of biologically active substances, and no special dietary products or food supplements are typically necessary. Food supplements, while helpful in some cases, provide only a small portion of the required micronutrients and cannot replace a balanced diet. Moreover, excessive use of supplements can lead to overdosing, especially when multiple formulations are used during pregnancy.

Vitamins and Mineral Formulations

Vitamin and mineral formulations available at pharmacies vary greatly in content and quantity of active substances. Many pregnancy-specific formulations contain excessive amounts of retinol (vitamin A) but insufficient folic acid, iodine, and other essential nutrients. It is crucial that pregnancy supplements do not contain retinol but include an appropriate amount of folic acid and other key nutrients.

If a pregnant woman has insufficient dietary calcium intake (e.g., due to low dairy consumption), she may require calcium supplements. However, retinol and vitamin A supplements should not be taken unless advised by a doctor.

When Supplements Are Needed?

Food supplements may be necessary in specific cases where dietary intake is insufficient or when there are special nutritional needs. Pregnant women who may require supplements include:

Women who are underweight or have nutritional disorders (e.g., anemia).

Women with a history of addiction (e.g., drugs or harmful substances).

Women with multiple consecutive pregnancies (especially those with birth intervals of less than 2 years).

Women who previously had a baby with low birth weight.

Women carrying multiple fetuses.

Medication During Pregnancy

Medications, prescription drugs, over-the-counter products, and food supplements should only be taken under strict medical supervision during pregnancy.

Maternal Diet and Allergy Prevention

There is no evidence suggesting that excluding specific foods during pregnancy or using prebiotics and probiotics can reduce the risk of allergies in offspring. In fact, unnecessary dietary restrictions could lead to insufficient intake of important nutrients. If the mother has a known allergy to certain foods, however, she should avoid them.

Vegetarian Diets During Pregnancy

Ovulate Vegetarians (who consume dairy products and eggs) can typically meet their nutritional needs through a well-balanced diet. The only supplements usually required are folic acid, iodine, and vitamin D. If fish is excluded, omega-3 fatty acids and docosahexaenoic acid (DHA) should also be included.

Vegetarians are at higher risk for iron deficiency and may need iron supplements more often. Additionally, women who have followed a vegetarian diet for an extended period before conception may be at greater risk for vitamin B12 and zinc deficiencies.

Pregnant vegetarians should consult with a nutritionist to ensure their diet is balanced and receive guidance on necessary supplements.

Vegan Diets During Pregnancy

Strict adherence to a vegan diet can pose significant health risks to both the mother and child, especially concerning the nervous system. Vegans are at risk for insufficient intake of energy, proteins, omega-3 fatty acids, calcium, iron, iodine, zinc, vitamin B12, and vitamin D. A vegan diet cannot be considered nutritionally complete without additional supplements. Pregnant vegans should consult with a dietitian or qualified nutritionist to receive personalized guidance and ensure proper supplementation throughout pregnancy.

Physical activity and Exercise during Pregnancy and Postpartum period

Exercise, defined as physical activity that involves planned, structured, and repetitive bodily movements aimed at improving one or more components of physical fitness, is an essential part of a healthy lifestyle. For women who were regularly engaged in vigorous-intensity aerobic activity or were physically active before pregnancy, it is generally safe to continue these activities during pregnancy and the postpartum period.

Studies have shown several benefits of exercise during pregnancy, including:

Reduced risk of gestational diabetes mellitus (diabetes during pregnancy).

Lower likelihood of cesarean delivery and operative vaginal delivery.

Faster postpartum recovery.

Reduced risk of depressive disorders during the postpartum period.

In the absence of obstetric or medical complications, and when no contraindications are present, physical activity during pregnancy is not only safe but also beneficial. Pregnant women should be encouraged to maintain or begin safe, moderate-intensity physical activities to support their health and well-being.

The Recent pieces of Evidence regarding the Benefits and Risks of Physical activity and Exercise during Pregnancy and the Postpartum period

Regular physical activity at all stages of life, including pregnancy, provides numerous health benefits. Pregnancy is an ideal time for maintaining or adopting a healthy lifestyle.

Physical activity and exercise during pregnancy are associated with minimal risks and have been shown to benefit most women. However, some modifications to exercise routines may be necessary due to the normal anatomical and physiological changes that occur during pregnancy, as well as fetal requirements. A thorough clinical evaluation should be conducted before recommending an exercise program to ensure that there are no medical contraindications to exercise.

Encouraging Physical Activity in Healthy Pregnancies:

Women with uncomplicated pregnancies should be encouraged to engage in aerobic and strength conditioning exercises both before, during, and after pregnancy. Obstetricians, gynecologists, and other healthcare providers should evaluate women with medical or obstetric complications carefully before making recommendations about physical activity during pregnancy.

Benefits of Physical Activity:

Physical activity, defined as any bodily movement produced by the contraction of skeletal muscles, plays a crucial role in maintaining and improving cardiorespiratory fitness. It also helps reduce the risk of obesity and associated comorbidities, ultimately contributing to greater longevity.

Promoting Healthy Lifestyles Before and During Pregnancy:

Women who begin their pregnancies with a healthy lifestyle should be encouraged to view the pre-pregnancy and pregnancy periods as opportunities to embrace healthier habits. Physical inactivity and excessive weight gain during pregnancy are recognized as independent risk factors for maternal obesity and related pregnancy complications. Therefore, adopting regular physical activity can help mitigate these risks.

Some examples of Exercise that have been extensively studied in Pregnancy and found to be Safe and Beneficial

The following forms of exercise are generally considered safe and beneficial during pregnancy:

Walking

Stationary Cycling

Aerobic Exercises

Dancing

Resistance Exercises

Stretching Exercises

Hydrotherapy

Water Aerobics

Benefits of Exercise During Pregnancy:

Engaging in regular physical activity during pregnancy has been shown to provide numerous benefits, including:

Higher incidence of normal or vaginal delivery

Lower incidence of excessive gestational weight gain

Reduced risk of gestational diabetes and gestational hypertension

Decreased likelihood of cesarean birth

Reduced risk of low birth weight

Prevention of depressive disorders

Relief from pain during the peripartum period

Individualized Exercise Plans:

While most expecting mothers can exercise safely, certain maternal medical conditions may require consultation with relevant specialists before engaging in aerobic exercise. For women with obstetric or medical comorbidities, exercise regimes should be tailored to their individual needs.

Effects of Exercise on Pregnancy

Pregnancy results in anatomic and physiologic changes (body changes) that should be considered before exercising.

The most distinct changes during pregnancy are weight gain and a shift in the point of gravity that results in **progressive lordosis**. (extensive inward curvature of the spine or curved spine in your back) it's normal to happen during pregnancy as the body shifts its angle to adjust space for the growing baby. These changes lead to an increase in the forces across joints and the spine during weight-bearing exercise. As a result, more than 60% of all pregnant women experience low back pain. Also, during rest posture is again important as both feet should be elevated.

During pregnancy there are a lot of changes occurring in the body like heart rate, blood volume, breathing rate, hormonal changes etc normally, exercise increases heart rate, and breathing rate, and also boosts some hormone secretion in the body, so it's necessary to consult your doctor to know how much exercise to do, when to do and how much rest is required after exercise, depending upon your body needs.

Again, during exercise temperature regulation and hydration is important, even if it is dependent on environmental conditions. During exercise, pregnant women should stay well hydrated, wear loose-fitting clothing and avoid high heat and humidity to protect against heat stress. Although exposure to heat from sources such as hot tubes, saunas, or fever has been associated with an increased risk of neural tube defects, exercise would not be expected to increase core body temperature into a range of concern. At least one study found no association between exercise and neural tube defects.

Most of the studies addressing foetal response to maternal exercise have found foetal heart rate and birth weight changes. Studies have shown there is a minimum to moderate increase in foetal heart rate by 10-30 beats per minute over the baseline during and after exercise. Differences in birth weight were minimal to none in women who exercised during pregnancy. However, women who had done vigorous exercise were more likely to deliver infants weighing 200-400g less than comparable controls, although there was not an increased risk of fetal growth restriction. so, we can conclude that the intensity of exercise should also be considered.

Warning Signs to Discontinue Exercise while Pregnant

Vaginal bleeding, abdominal pain, regular painful contractions, amniotic fluid leakage, dyspnoea before exertion, dizziness, headache, chest pain, muscle weakness affecting balance, calf pain or swelling, if observed stop exercising and consult your doctor immediately.

Pregnant women who were sedentary before pregnancy should follow a more gradual progression of exercise. And women who were regularly exercising before pregnancy and who have uncomplicated, healthy pregnancies can continue their exercise programmes, that to within a limit.

High-intensity or prolonged exercise over 45 minutes can lead to hypoglycaemia (reduced glucose level); therefore, adequate calorie intake before exercising or limiting the intensity or length of exercise session, is essential to minimize this risk.

Types of Exercise Depending on you-

Women with uncomplicated pregnancies should be encouraged to engage in aerobic and strength-conditioning exercises before, during and after pregnancy. Activities with a high risk of abdominal trauma or imbalance should be avoided, scuba diving should also be avoided in pregnancy.

According to studies, women living at sea level were better able to tolerate physical activity up to altitudes of 6,000 feet, suggesting this altitude is safe in pregnancy, although more research is needed. Women who reside in higher altitudes may be able to exercise safely at altitudes higher than 6,000 feet.

In those instances, in which women experience low back pain, exercising in water is an alternative. A study of apparent weight reduction during water immersion was seen in the third trimester (last three months of pregnancy) a reduction that lowers the maternal osteoarticular load due to buoyancy. There may be additional benefits of aquatic exercises as well. A randomized controlled trial of an aquatic physical exercise program during pregnancy consisting of three 60 minutes exercises has demonstrated a greater rate of intact perineum (skin between your genitals and anus) after childbirth.

Special population

Pregnant women with obesity should be encouraged to engage in healthy lifestyle modification during pregnancy that includes physical activity and judicious diets. Vigorous-intensity exercise completed into the third trimester appears to be safe for most healthy pregnancies, further research is needed on the effects of vigorous-intensity exercise in the second and first trimesters and of exercise intensity exceeding 90% of maximum heart rate.

Competitive athletes require frequent and close supervision because they tend to maintain a more strenuous training schedule throughout pregnancy and resume high-intensity training postpartum(after giving birth) sooner than other women. Such athletes should pay particular attention to avoiding hyperthermia, maintaining proper hydration and sustaining adequate calorie intake to prevent weight loss, which may adversely affect foetal growth.

Several reviews have determined that there is no credible evidence to prescribe bed rest in pregnancy for the prevention of preterm labour, and it should not be routinely recommended. Little or basic physical activity can be included unless the case is complex.

According to studies on occupational exposure such as long working hours, shift work, lifting, standing and physical workload during pregnancy leads to preterm delivery, low birth weight, preeclampsia and gestational hypertension (abnormal BP during pregnancy). so, it's advised to avoid occupational workload as much as possible.

Exercise in the Postpartum (after Childbirth) period-

Several reports indicate that women's level of participation in exercise programs diminishes after childbirth, leading to being overweight and obese. Resuming exercise or incorporating new exercise routines after delivery is important in supporting lifelong healthy habits. Exercise routines may be resumed gradually as soon as medically safe, depending on the mode of delivery and the presence or absence of medical or surgical complications.

Pelvic floor exercises can be initiated in the immediate postpartum period. Abdominal strengthening exercises, including abdominal crunch exercises and the drawing-in exercise, a manoeuvre (a movement that requires care or skill) that increases abdominal pressure by pulling in the abdominal wall muscles, have been shown to decrease the incidence of Diastases Recti (abdominal separation) and decrease the inter rectus distance in women who gave birth vaginally or by caesarean birth. Regular aerobic exercise in lactating women has been shown to improve maternal cardiovascular fitness without affecting milk production, composition or infant growth. Women who are lactating should consider feeding their infants or expressing milk before exercising to avoid the discomfort of engorged breasts. They need to ensure adequate hydration before commencing physical activity.

Spiritualism During Pregnancy

In simple words, spiritual pregnancy is the process of developing wisdom in the soul.

What is spirituality?

Spirituality is a deeply personal journey, focused on finding meaning, purpose, and connection in life. While it may or may not involve religion, it offers a sense of faith, hope, peace, and empowerment. The practice of spirituality can lead to joy, forgiveness, self-awareness, acceptance of hardship, a deeper sense of well-being, and the ability to transcend life's challenges.

Spirituality encompasses a broad belief in something beyond the self. It may be tied to religious traditions that center around a higher power, but it can also involve a holistic connection to others and the world. It suggests that life holds more than what is physically experienced, offering a worldview that connects all beings to the universe. It often provides answers to existential questions about life's meaning, human connections, and the mysteries of existence, including the belief in an ongoing existence after death.

Research has shown that engaging in spiritual practices can offer comfort and relief from stress. Those who rely on spirituality to cope with life's challenges tend to experience benefits such as improved health and overall well-being. Spirituality is not confined to one belief system; it's an individual experience that can manifest in many ways.

Some may turn to religion, while others find connection through nature, relationships, or personal growth.

Signs of Spirituality:

Asking deep existential questions (e.g., suffering, life after death)

Developing stronger connections with others

Experiencing empathy and compassion

Feeling a sense of interconnectedness with the world

Seeking happiness beyond material possessions

Desiring purpose and meaning in life

Aiming to make the world a better place

Spiritual experiences vary greatly from person to person. Some may find spiritual meaning in their religious practices, while others experience it in nature or in moments of deep reflection. Spirituality can be expressed through many traditions such as Hinduism, Buddhism, Christianity, Islam, Judaism, Sikhism, Humanism, and New Age spirituality, among others.

Why People Turn to Spirituality?:

People explore spirituality for a variety of reasons, including:

Finding Purpose and Meaning: Seeking answers to life's philosophical questions.

Coping with Stress, Depression, and Anxiety: Spirituality can provide solace and a sense of peace during difficult times.

Restoring Hope and Optimism: Spiritual practices can foster a more positive outlook on life.

Finding Community and Support: Many spiritual traditions offer a sense of belonging and support through organized groups.

Health Benefits of Spirituality: Research highlights several positive effects of spirituality on physical and mental health:

Spirituality can help cope with everyday stress, leading to better emotional regulation and positive feelings.

Studies show that individuals with a strong intrinsic religious orientation often experience lower physiological stress responses and better physical health.

Spiritual practices like prayer have been linked to improved psychological well-being, lower levels of depression, hypertension, and stress, and an enhanced ability to handle life's challenges.

Spirituality offers profound benefits for mental and physical health, providing individuals with the tools to navigate life's complexities with a sense of purpose, peace, and resilience.

Importance of spiritual pregnancy

Motherhood is a transformative experience that involves significant physical, psychological, and social changes for women. During this period, social support plays a crucial role in helping women navigate the challenges of pregnancy, childbirth, and postpartum adaptation. It has been shown that social support during pregnancy is associated with better mental health outcomes and a reduced likelihood of postpartum depression. In particular, support from family and close relationships can act as a protective factor, fostering resilience and life satisfaction.

Social support can have a direct and indirect impact on a woman's mental well-being. Directly, it enhances life satisfaction by providing emotional and practical assistance. Indirectly, it serves as a buffer against the negative effects of stress and distress, promoting better mental adaptation during pregnancy and after childbirth. A woman's ability to accept the role of motherhood and adapt to the changes brought on by pregnancy is influenced by the support she receives, as well as her personal characteristics and the care provided by midwives and healthcare professionals.

Life satisfaction is closely linked to social, economic, family, and personal factors. Discrepancies between a person's goals, desires, and needs, often exacerbated by stress or workload, can lead to dissatisfaction. Social support can mitigate the effects of stress, helping individuals maintain a positive outlook on life and improving their overall well-being.

Spiritual Well-being and Life Satisfaction: Spiritual well-being is an important aspect of overall life satisfaction and is often studied in terms of two dimensions: religious spirituality and spirituality of existence. Religious spirituality refers to the connection with a higher power or ultimate reality, while spirituality of existence relates to psychological experiences that do not necessarily involve religious beliefs. Both dimensions contribute to a sense of purpose, happiness, inner peace, and positive attitude, all of which enhance life satisfaction.

Spiritual well-being is considered an essential component of health-related quality of life. Without spiritual well-being, achieving a balanced and fulfilling life is challenging. Increasing one's sense of meaning and purpose through spiritual practices can help individuals overcome life's challenges and improve their overall life satisfaction.

The concept of "holism" suggests that a person is not merely a physical being, but an integrated whole of body, mind, and spirit. The mind-body-spirit connection emphasizes the importance of addressing all aspects of a person's health and well-being. The spirit, often seen as the essence of a person, plays a central role in defining one's identity and overall health. Humanistic interpretations of spirituality tend to focus on the individual's internal sense of self rather than religious terms like "soul." Ensuring care for the spirit is therefore essential for maintaining overall well-being.

In summary, the integration of physical, emotional, social, and spiritual aspects of health is key to fostering a healthy, fulfilling life, particularly during the transformative experience of motherhood.

Social support, spiritual well-being, and holistic care are all critical components that contribute to a woman's mental health and life satisfaction during pregnancy and beyond.

Proofs, Research and Surveys Done on Spiritual Pregnancy-

I have referred to various researches, surveys and concluded the observations and results.

Spirituality often refers to an integrated and ever-evolving concept that transcends our ability to fully define or structure it. This fluidity does not negate its existence but instead invites deeper reflection, particularly when exploring the profound gifts childbirth offers.

Many women have shared that childbirth was a moment of deep spiritual connection. For some, it was a time to feel closer to the divine. One woman from the Mormon faith described her experience as follows: "The nurse was cheering me on loudly, but as the baby was born, everything went silent. The nurse, doctor, and my husband all became quiet. It felt as though time stood still, and the room became bright. In that moment, I felt the spirit's presence."

A Guatemalan mother echoed a similar sentiment, stating, "Giving birth brought me closer to God. I thanked Him for the gift of my baby. During my pregnancy, I marveled at God's greatness, realizing only He could watch over the child in my womb."

Another Mormon woman described the holiness she felt during childbirth: "When my baby was born, I felt the Lord's spirit touch my heart. I understood that this innocent soul had come from my Heavenly Father. I felt immense gratitude for the blessing of being a woman and for the role I played in bringing a child from heaven to earth."

For a Canadian Orthodox Jewish mother, childbirth was the ultimate mitzvah—a good deed of immense spiritual significance. She shared, "You feel God's presence most tangibly after going through childbirth." Similarly, an Arabic Muslim woman described a profound sense of unity with God during labour: "During childbirth, I was in God's hands. Each night of my pregnancy, I recited verses from the Qur'an for my baby. In labour, I read a special prayer for protection. The nurses were moved to tears. It felt like a miracle was unfolding—a holy presence surrounding me as part of God's creation."

Some women described childbirth as a spiritual journey without necessarily associating it with formal religious faith. For example, a Chinese mother acknowledged the sacredness of the experience, saying, "Every mother endures pain, but I believe it is a sacred process." A Finnish woman emphasized the importance of inner balance, advising, "Each mother should listen to her body, remain calm, and accept what comes."

Religious Beliefs and Rituals as Coping Mechanisms

Religious practices often served as vital coping mechanisms for women during labor. A Tongan woman shared how her faith sustained her: "When the pain was at its worst, I called out to God for help. I cried out, 'Jesus, help me,' and felt that God was saving me as I gave birth."

Many women also reported that their spiritual practices became more meaningful during pregnancy and childbirth. A Tongan woman expressed, "Pregnancy is a time for spiritual growth, so the baby can be created with goodness." An Evangelical Christian mother of five emphasized the importance of gratitude, saying, "The Lord's spirit helped me, and I gave thanks to Him for this blessing."

Faith in a Higher Power and Positive Birth Outcomes

For many women, belief in a higher power was central to their pregnancy and birth experiences, especially in regions where maternal and infant mortality rates are high. A Mexican immigrant mother shared, "I prayed to God to protect me and my baby. My child was born healthy because God listened to my prayers."

A Ghanaian mother of twins, who had experienced a prior loss, said, "I wasn't afraid. I left everything to God." She reflected on the delicate balance of life and death during childbirth, adding, "This is a time when I need God's spiritual protection."

Childbirth as a Spiritually Transformative Experience

For many, childbirth was a deeply transformative experience. A Finnish mother described the birth of her first child as a rebirth for herself, marking her transition into motherhood. A South African woman likened the spiritual transformation of giving birth to her experiences in church, saying, "The baby comes from heaven."

Similarly, a Muslim mother reflected, "This pregnancy reminded me of God's ability to create life. My faith grew stronger."

Providing Spiritual Care During Childbirth

Understanding the spiritual aspects of childbirth enables healthcare providers to offer more holistic care. Spiritual care involves presence, active listening, and helping women articulate their feelings about their experiences. This goes beyond evidence-based practices to foster trust, connection, and respect.

To support a woman's spiritual needs, caregivers might ask, "Do you have any spiritual beliefs that could help us provide better care during your pregnancy and childbirth?" After the birth, asking, "What was your experience like?" allows women to reflect on the spiritual dimensions of their journey, offering a chance to honour and express the profound emotions associated with this transformative event.

Childbirth and motherhood offer profound opportunities to explore the spiritual dimensions of a woman's life. These experiences foster a deep connection to all aspects of existence, transcending linear or cyclical notions of time. The period surrounding childbirth often feels like a shared, temporal phenomenon that links past, present, and future generations. This extraordinary period, sometimes described as "Kairos time," is perceived as a sacred moment where the visible and invisible merge, evoking a sense of divinity and holiness—even in unexpected and high-risk situations.

Women who face challenging childbirth experiences often turn to spiritual practices as a source of recovery and integration. Rather than relying on predetermined processes to evoke spirituality, it is the attunement to the unique spiritual essence of birth that reveals its deeper significance. Birth is more than a physical event; it carries a profound, intangible quality that can evoke emotions such as awe, joy, and wonder, deeply felt by all present. These moments—tears of happiness, sudden smiles, or a sense of the extraordinary—highlight the spiritual resonance of childbirth, which profoundly impacts women and those supporting them, including midwives.

Midwives' Perspectives on Spirituality

In discussions with midwives, spirituality emerged as a concept deeply intertwined with their practice. While not necessarily tied to religious beliefs, it was described as an intrinsic part of their role—rooted in care, connection, and understanding. Spiritual and holistic care, as midwives expressed, involves building meaningful relationships with women, respecting cultural and religious needs, and approaching each individual without judgment.

Midwives observed that pregnant women often seemed to draw strength from an internal or external spiritual source, though its nature was sometimes difficult to articulate. This strength enabled women to navigate even the most challenging childbirth experiences.

Spirituality in High-Risk Pregnancies

Research has shown that spirituality plays a vital role in helping women cope with complicated or high-risk pregnancies. In a study of women facing such challenges, most participants associated spirituality with religion, whether they actively participated in religious communities or not. All participants acknowledged a connection with something transcendent or sacred and shared that in times of crisis, they reached out more fervently to this presence.

Many women expressed their spirituality through religious practices such as attending church, prayer, and adhering to the values of their faith traditions. Others used spiritual language to describe their experiences without aligning with specific religious frameworks, speaking instead of "souls," "energies," or "spirits" that they believed were present within and around them.

For some, spirituality was expressed in non-religious terms, focusing on relationships, emotions, and personal connections. These women found spiritual meaning in activities like spending time in nature, journaling, caring for animals, nurturing relationships, or living a life guided by moral principles.

The Therapeutic Power of Spiritual Dialogue

Many women reported that engaging in spiritual dialogue provided therapeutic benefits. Before prayer or spiritual practices, participants often described feelings of anxiety, confusion, or nervousness. However, during and after these interactions, they reported a renewed sense of calm, reassurance, and confidence. Spiritual practices gave them strength, peace, and a positive outlook they hadn't experienced before.

Several women noted that discussing their spirituality during difficult times helped them better understand its influence in their lives. These conversations brought comfort and reassurance, offering a level of emotional support that even close family and friends could not provide.

The Impact of Spirituality on Stress and Mental Health

The emotional and physical challenges of pregnancy can increase stress, which may negatively impact the health of both mother and baby. For pregnant women living with HIV, this stress is often compounded by guilt, fear of transmission, and societal stigma. Research indicates that up to 40% of HIV-positive pregnant women experience mental health disorders. Partner and family support are critical in helping these women manage their stress and emotional discomfort.

Studies have also highlighted the significant positive impact of self-compassion and spirituality on reducing depression during pregnancy. Self-compassion, which involves being kind to oneself, recognizing shared human struggles, and maintaining emotional balance, was found to reduce self-criticism and contribute nearly 20% to improved mental health outcomes. Spirituality provided an additional 10% benefit, demonstrating its importance in fostering resilience and emotional well-being during pregnancy.

Implementation of Methods of Application of Spiritualism during Pregnancy

Meditation-

Meditation can offer significant benefits during pregnancy, especially in managing the stress and physical discomforts that often accompany this life-changing event. It is known to reduce symptoms like fatigue, mood swings, and sleep disturbances, while also lowering anxiety and depression. Here are some forms of meditation that can be particularly beneficial:

Mindfulness Meditation: Focus on the present moment, paying attention to physical and emotional sensations without judgment.

Transcendental Meditation: Involves silently repeating a mantra to quiet the mind.

Walking Meditation: Combines mindful walking with breathing awareness.

Body Scanning: Focus on relaxing specific muscle groups in the body to reduce tension.

Deep Breathing: Focused, rhythmic breathing helps relax the nervous system and reduces muscle tension.

Progressive Muscle Relaxation: Involves tensing and relaxing muscle groups, promoting relaxation and reducing stress.

Guided Imagery: Visualizing a peaceful and relaxing place can help reduce stress and anxiety.

Loving-Kindness Meditation: Cultivates feelings of compassion and kindness, promoting emotional well-being.

Mantra Meditation: Repeating a mantra or phrase to calm the mind.

Benefits:

Reduces anxiety, depression, and perceived stress.

Improves sleep and reduces pregnancy symptoms.

May ease labor pain by promoting relaxation and enhancing the perception of pain.

Supports mental well-being during the emotional transitions of pregnancy.

Yoga and Pranayama-

Yoga, a mind-body practice originating in India, combines physical postures (asanas), controlled breathing (pranayama), and meditation. Pranayama, or yogic breathing, is particularly beneficial for improving oxygen intake and calming the mind.

Benefits of Yoga:

Prepares the body for labor by improving flexibility, strength, and endurance.

Reduces common pregnancy discomforts like nausea, constipation, and back pain.

Promotes emotional balance and mental clarity.

Strengthens the muscles, especially the core and pelvic area, aiding in smoother childbirth.

Key Yoga Poses for Pregnancy:

Butterfly Pose: Improves abdominal function and promotes smoother delivery.

Trikonasana (Triangle Pose): Strengthens the hips, back, and legs while reducing stress and anxiety.

Bhramari Pranayama: Helps release agitation and frustration, calming the mind.

Anulom-Vilom Pranayama: A balancing breathing technique that reduces stress and anxiety.

Bhastrika Pranayama: Improves focus, removes toxins, and supports overall health.

Benefits of Pranayama:

Helps calm the nervous system.

Promotes relaxation and reduces anxiety.

Improves oxygenation and energy levels.

Prepares the body for the challenges of labor.

Nurture Your Connection with Your Baby-

Building a strong emotional connection with your baby can be incredibly fulfilling during pregnancy. This connection helps foster feelings of joy, peace, and love, creating a positive bond between mother and child.

Ways to Nurture Your Connection:

Talking and Singing: Speak or sing to your baby, even if they can't yet respond verbally.

Reading: Read aloud to your baby, which can create a soothing environment.

Listening to Music: Play calming music to relax both you and your baby.

Belly Massage: Gently massage your belly, creating a sense of warmth and closeness.

Mindful Breathing: Focus on deep, calming breaths while connecting with your baby, feeling the breath surrounding them.

Benefits:

Strengthens the emotional bond between mother and baby.

Promotes relaxation and emotional well-being.

Reduces stress and fosters a positive mindset during pregnancy.

Enhances the experience of pregnancy, helping to manage physical and emotional changes.

Integrating meditation, yoga, pranayama, and emotional nurturing into your daily routine can significantly improve your overall health and well-being during pregnancy. These practices help to manage stress, enhance physical and mental strength, and build a deeper connection with your baby, ultimately supporting a smoother pregnancy and a more positive birth experience.

As with any new practice, especially during pregnancy, it's important to consult with your healthcare provider before beginning new exercises or meditation techniques to ensure they are safe for your individual health needs.

Spiritual Beliefs and Practices According to Your Religion and Culture

Depending on your social, religious and cultural background you may have certain needs and expectations when you are having a baby. Different cultures have different values, beliefs and practices. A woman's cultural background can affect her needs and expectations during pregnancy and childbirth as well as how she and her family raise children.

Food taboos have a big influence on pregnant women as they have been followed by many generations and they also form part of their culture. Consequently, people practising these pregnancy-related taboos believe that breaking them may harm the unborn baby or threaten the health of the mother. Additional reasons for a woman to avoid certain foods include their fear of possible miscarriage and difficulties during delivery. Some women observe these food taboos because it is a symbol of respect for elders. This avoidance of food usually does not conform to the medical view about the appropriate types and quantity of foods needed by pregnant women to safeguard the ideal maternal fetal nutrition. Traditional beliefs may influence women to disobey recommendations or advice from health care practitioners. So its better to make wise decisions regarding health of your baby.

Garbh Sanskar: An Age old Tradition or Science, Where Mothers Can Shape Their Baby in the Womb

Garbh Sanskar is about creating a positive and nurturing environment for the baby while they are still in the womb. It means teaching good things and values to your unborn child by focusing on your thoughts, feelings, and actions during pregnancy.

How the Baby Develops in the Womb

The Baby Can Sense Things Early:

Babies can start hearing from the 5th month of pregnancy.

They respond to sounds, emotions, and even your thoughts!

Brain Growth:

80% of the baby's brain develops in the womb.

The brain forms connections for emotions, memory, learning, and senses like hearing, touch, and vision.

Your Influence on the Baby:

The baby is affected by your mood, diet, and thoughts.

Positive actions can help the baby grow smarter, healthier, and happier.

Why Your Emotions Matter?

Happy Mom = Happy Baby:

When you're happy, your body produces hormones like serotonin and endorphins, which make the baby feel calm and loved.

Listening to soothing music or reading positive stories creates these happy feelings.

Stress Affects the Baby:

If you're stressed, your body releases hormones like cortisol that can make the baby feel anxious or sad.

Long-term stress can lead to babies being born with lower confidence or a timid personality.

How to Practice Garbh Sanskar?

1. Meditation:

Spend 15-20 minutes daily sitting quietly and relaxing your mind.

Imagine your baby and send them loving, happy thoughts.

You can do this in a peaceful room with soft music or pleasant scents.

2. Music for the Baby:

Play calming music like classical tunes, ragas, or chants.

The baby responds to music, and it helps in brain development.

Examples: Veena, flute, sitar, or mantras like the Gayatri Mantra.

3. Talk and Bond with Your Baby:

Talk, sing, and read to your baby.

Rub your belly gently and respond to their kicks.

Your voice creates a sense of comfort and security for them.

4. Eat a Healthy Diet:

Eat fresh, balanced meals with all tastes: sweet, sour, salty, bitter, and more.

Avoid junk food and focus on home-cooked meals that are nutritious.

5. Stay Active:

Do light yoga or go for short walks.

These activities keep you fit and improve blood flow to the baby.

Why It's Important?

The Mental Umbilical Cord:

Just like the umbilical cord gives your baby food and oxygen, your emotions and thoughts also reach the baby.

Positive feelings create a healthy, happy baby.

Shape Your Baby's Future:

Babies exposed to positive stimuli in the womb grow up smarter, calmer, and more confident.

Your actions now can influence their personality and health for life.

Tips for Everyday Garbh Sanskar:

Start your day with a positive mindset. Meditate or listen to peaceful music.

Avoid watching violent or stressful TV shows.

Read uplifting stories, holy texts, or inspiring books.

Take breaks to relax and enjoy small things like nature or art.

Share your feelings with loved ones to stay emotionally balanced.

By practicing Garbh Sanskar, you're not just taking care of yourself—you're also giving your baby the best start in life. Remember, a happy mom leads to a happy baby!

Practical Aspects of Pregnancy

Things to avoid during pregnancy

Foods to avoid during pregnancy-

 Dairy Products:

Foods to Enjoy:

Pasteurized or unpasteurized hard cheeses like Cheddar, Gruyere, and Parmesan.

Pasteurized semi-soft cheeses like Edam and Stilton.

Pasteurized soft cheeses such as Cottage cheese, Mozzarella, Feta, Cream cheese, Paneer, Ricotta, Halloumi, and Goat's cheese (without a white rind).

Processed cheese spreads.

Soft or blue cheeses (pasteurized or unpasteurized) that are cooked until steaming hot.

Pasteurized Milk, Yogurt, Cream, and Ice cream.

Foods to Avoid:

Unpasteurized milk-based products, like soft-ripened Goat's cheese.

Mould-ripened soft cheeses with a white rind (Brie, Camembert, Chèvre) unless cooked thoroughly.

Soft blue cheeses like Danish blue, Gorgonzola, and Roquefort unless cooked thoroughly.

Unpasteurized Cow's, Goat's, or Sheep's Milk and Cream.

Why:

There's a risk of Listeriosis from unpasteurized or soft-ripened dairy, which could harm the baby, leading to complications like miscarriage or stillbirth. Soft cheeses with a white coating may allow bacteria to grow more easily. Cooking these cheeses kills harmful bacteria.

Meats & Poultry:

Foods to Enjoy:

Well-cooked meats such as Chicken, Pork, and Beef (ensure no pink or blood).

Cold, pre-packed meats like Ham and Corned Beef.

Foods to Be Cautious With:

Cold-cured meats like Salami, Pepperoni, Chorizo, and Prosciutto (only if cooked thoroughly).

Foods to Avoid:

Raw or undercooked meat, Liver, and liver products.

Game meats like Goose, Partridge, or Pheasant.

Why:

Raw or undercooked meats may carry Toxoplasmosis, which can increase the risk of miscarriage. Cured meats may contain parasites, and liver products are high in vitamin A, which could harm the baby. Game meats might contain lead shot.

Eggs:

Foods to Avoid:

Dishes with raw or undercooked eggs (unless pasteurized).

Raw or undercooked eggs in restaurant dishes.

Deli items made with eggs, like deviled eggs and egg salad, unless they are cooked thoroughly and fresh.

Soft-boiled, poached, or runny eggs, and dishes made with raw eggs (like homemade mayonnaise, ice cream, and batter).

Why:

Raw or undercooked eggs can carry Salmonella, which can cause food poisoning. Since pregnancy weakens the immune system, it's safer to consume only pasteurized or fully cooked eggs.

Fish:

Foods to Enjoy:

Well-cooked fish and seafood, including shellfish like Mussels, Lobster, Crab, Prawns, Scallops, and Clams.

Foods to Be Cautious With:

Smoked fish (only eat if thoroughly cooked).

Why:

Smoked fish may contain Listeria, which can lead to infection. Cook smoked fish thoroughly to reduce the risk.

Foods to Limit:

No more than two servings of oily fish per week (e.g., Salmon, Mackerel, Herring) and limit Tuna consumption due to mercury content.

Foods to Avoid:

Swordfish, Marlin, Shark, and raw shellfish due to higher mercury levels and potential toxins in raw shellfish.

Other Foods & Drinks:

Caffeine:

Limit to 200mg per day (roughly 1-2 cups of coffee).

Alcohol:

Avoid alcohol completely during pregnancy due to potential risks to the baby.

Herbal Teas:

Limit to no more than four cups per day.

Liquorice:

Safe in moderation, but avoid liquorice root.

Peanuts:

No need to avoid unless you have a nut allergy.

Vitamins:

Avoid high-dose multivitamins containing vitamin A unless prescribed by a doctor.

Raw Sprouts:

Avoid raw sprouts due to risk of E. coli or Salmonella contamination.

Unwashed Produce:

Always wash fruits and vegetables thoroughly to reduce the risk of bacterial infections like Listeria or Salmonella.

Smoking:

Avoid smoking and secondhand smoke to prevent pregnancy complications.

Recreational Drugs:

Avoid illegal drugs, and consult your doctor for guidance and support.

Acupuncture and Massage:

Generally safe but avoid abdominal massage in the first trimester. Consult with a qualified practitioner.

Cats:

Avoid handling cat litter to reduce the risk of Toxoplasmosis.

Cleaning Products:

Ensure proper ventilation and follow safety instructions for cleaning products.

Fake Tan:

Safe to use but be cautious of skin sensitivity changes during pregnancy.

Hair Dye:

Safe in moderation, but with precautions like using gloves and proper ventilation.

Painting:

Minimize exposure to fumes and lead-based paint, especially in the first trimester.

Saunas and Jacuzzis:

Avoid due to the risk of overheating.

Sunbeds:

Avoid due to the risk of skin cancer and potential folate depletion.

X-rays:

Minimize exposure, and consult your healthcare provider to assess the risks during pregnancy.

Things to do during Pregnancy

Folic Acid Supplementation

Taking folic acid significantly reduces the risk of neural tube defects, such as spina bifida. It's recommended to begin taking 400 micrograms of folic acid daily as soon as possible, continuing through the first trimester (up to week 12). Some individuals, like those with diabetes or epilepsy, may need a higher dose. This helps with the development of healthy bones, teeth, and muscles for your baby.

Eat a Balanced Diet

Eating a variety of foods is essential for both your energy and your baby's growth. Include fruits, vegetables, meats, cheese, potatoes, beans, and pulses in your diet. If you're having trouble maintaining a healthy diet, consult with a doctor or dietitian for guidance.

Stay Active

Physical activity during pregnancy is beneficial for both mother and baby. It helps improve sleep, reduce anxiety, and maintain overall health. If you were active before pregnancy, continue with caution. If not, aim for 30 minutes of moderate activity each day, such as walking.

Avoid Certain Activities

While most exercises are safe during pregnancy, avoid activities like diving and contact sports, as they may pose risks to you and your baby.

Monitor Your Baby's Movements

Fetal movements are a sign of a healthy pregnancy. Typically, movements are felt between 18 and 24 weeks, starting as gentle fluttering and progressing to kicks. If you notice any significant changes in movement patterns, consult with your healthcare provider.

Sleep on Your Side in the Third Trimester

Sleeping on your side, particularly during the final trimester, is recommended to reduce risks to both you and your baby. If you wake up on your back, gently shift back to your side.

Take Care of Your Mental Health

Pregnancy can bring emotional changes. It's normal to experience mood swings, but if feelings of sadness or anxiety persist, seek support from a healthcare provider. Many women experience mental health challenges during pregnancy or in the year following birth.

Vaccinations During Pregnancy

Certain vaccinations are recommended to protect both you and your baby. The whooping cough vaccine is advised between 16 and 32 weeks of pregnancy to safeguard your baby until they can receive their own vaccinations. The flu vaccine is also recommended, especially during flu season, to prevent complications during pregnancy.

Carry Your Pregnancy Notes

Keep your antenatal notes with you at all times, as they contain important medical information. This is especially useful if you need emergency care.

Prepare for Travel

If travelling abroad, ensure your travel insurance covers pregnancy-related issues. Long trips may increase the risk of blood clots, so wear compression stockings, stay hydrated, and move regularly. Check with airlines for their policies if flying after 28 weeks.

Know the Red Flags

Certain symptoms require immediate medical attention, such as vaginal bleeding, painful urination, severe headaches, or changes in baby movements. Trust your instincts and seek help if something feels off.

Get Plenty of Rest

Adequate sleep is essential, particularly in the final trimester. Aim for 7-9 hours of sleep per night, and take naps as needed to rest and recharge.

Practice Gentle Yoga

Prenatal or gentle yoga classes can be beneficial during pregnancy. Avoid high-intensity yoga, and always consult with your doctor before starting a class if you weren't practicing yoga before pregnancy.

Manage Weight Gain

While it's common to gain weight during pregnancy, it's important to do so gradually and healthily. The first trimester requires minimal extra calories, but by the third trimester, you'll need around 300-500 additional calories per day.

Enjoy Occasional Cravings

Pregnancy cravings are common and can be a response to nutritional needs or emotional factors. It's okay to indulge occasionally, but be mindful of portion sizes and avoid foods that pose a risk, like raw meat or unpasteurized cheeses.

Practical Aspects of Pregnancy

When you are pregnant, your baby changes every day, and your body keeps pace. Here is some information about week-by-week progress including some interesting facts and tests to be done during this period.

First Trimester

Week 1 and 2

Your pregnancy journey starts now, even though you're not technically pregnant yet. Most healthcare providers count pregnancy from the first day of your last menstrual period. During these weeks, your body is preparing for ovulation and fertilization, which typically occurs in week 3.

Tips: Take folic acid supplements.

Consult your doctor about medications.

Be mindful of early pregnancy symptoms.

Week 3

Congratulations, you've conceived! You're now in the first month of your pregnancy, though it may take a few weeks to confirm with a test. The tiny cluster of cells is growing rapidly, and hormonal changes might give you a heightened sense of smell. This is due to hormones like estrogen and hCG.

Baby's Size: Vanilla bean seed.

Tips: Start iron and vitamin C supplements.

Eat calcium-rich foods and protein.

And be cautious not to lift heavy objects, and be careful while walking, sitting not to put pressure on your abdomen, and even be cautious with kids as they may hit on your abdomen and don't lift them.

Spend at least two hours a day by speaking with your child and pampering your womb. This creates a bond between you both. And also imagine how you want your baby to be- physically, mentally and behaviour wise.

Week 4

Your body is forming the placenta and amniotic sac. You may notice mild abdominal pressure, tender breasts, or even implantation bleeding. Symptoms like mood swings and bloating may also appear.

Baby's Size: Poppy seed.

Tips: Take vitamin D and omega-3 fatty acids.

Avoid smoking and second-hand smoke.

Schedule your first prenatal appointment.

Try a new comfort food, make a prenatal appointment, and avoid foods that cause allergy and food poisoning.

Week 5

You're now in the second month! hCG levels are high enough to confirm pregnancy with a test. Symptoms like nausea, fatigue, and food aversions may start.

Baby's Size: Orange seed.

Tips: Avoid cleaning cat litter.

Increase your protein intake.

Manage bloating with a balanced diet.

Week 6

Your baby's head, cheeks, chin, and jaws are beginning to form. You may experience heartburn, nausea, and frequent urination.

Baby's Size: Sweet pea.

Tips: for frequent urination, lean forward when you pee to ensure that your bladder is completely empty each time.

Suffering from morning sickness have dry cereal, pretzels, rice cakes, well-toasted bread and breadsticks, better keep them on your bedside table, never sleep with an empty stomach at least have these to prevent acid production that leads to heartburn and nausea.

Try to avoid foods like citruses and tomatoes, greasy and spicy foods, and don't rush through your meals and avoid clothes that constrict your belly. It's a good idea to finish dinner at least four hours before going to bed and keep your head elevated on a pillow while you sleep, this somewhat prevents heartburn and indigestion.

Don't skip all seafood, just avoid high-mercury fish, look out for urinary tract infection symptoms, start the workout and pamper yourself.

Week 7

Your baby is developing new brain cells at an astonishing rate. The umbilical cord is fully formed, connecting the baby to the placenta.

Baby's Size: Blueberry.

Tips: Safely manage skincare products.

Monitor your weight and abdominal cramps.

know what to avoid and how much to avoid during pregnancy(refer back).

Week 8

Though you may not be showing yet, your clothes might feel tighter. The baby's lips, eyelids, and nose are forming.

Baby's Size: Raspberry.

Tips: Eat six small meals daily instead of three large ones.

Ease into a light exercise routine.

Week 9

Your body is working hard to develop the placenta, your baby's lifeline.

Baby's Size: Green olive.

Tips: Include fiber-rich foods in your diet.

Sleep on your side for better blood flow.

Week 10

Your baby transitions from an embryo to a fetus, and their tiny elbows and cartilage are forming. Visible veins and increased vaginal discharge may appear.

Baby's Size: Prune.

Tips: Avoid strong smells that trigger nausea.

Add mangoes to your diet for vitamins A and C.

Week 11

Your baby now has distinct human features like fingers and toes. Morning sickness might ease for some, though symptoms like bloating and food cravings may persist.

Baby's Size: Large strawberry.

Tips: Begin prenatal yoga.

Stay clean to avoid infections. At this stage, your immune system is working at a lower speed than usual which is a good thing since it keeps your growing baby protected and stops your body from fighting the fetus off as a foreign body. The downside- your body can't ward off colds as well as it normally does, making you more vulnerable to cough and cold, so better take care as you can't take medicines during pregnancy, and learn about NT screening-Nuchal translucency screening.

Week 12

This week marks the formation of key body systems and vital organs. Your baby's bone marrow is producing white blood cells to fight germs.

Baby's Size: Lime.

Tips: Stay hydrated and get your flu vaccine.

Avoid hair removal treatments.

If you feel dizzy or faint, lie down or sit with your head lowered between your knees, take deep breaths and loosen any tight clothing. As soon as you feel a little better, get something to eat or drink.

Week 13

Tiny bones are forming in the baby's arms and legs, and movement begins. As you approach the second trimester, symptoms like bloating, constipation, and headaches may persist for some.

Baby's Size: Lemon.

Tips: Continue prenatal vitamins.

Include iron and fiber-rich foods in your meals.

Second trimester

Week 14:

Baby Development: Hair growth begins, including eyebrows and a downy layer called lanugo. The digestive system produces meconium, which is the waste that will make up their first bowel movement after birth.

Baby Size: As big as a navel orange.

Tips: Start light exercise, avoid tattoos, and eat fresh foods. And be cautious not to lift heavy objects, and be careful while walking, and sitting not to put pressure on your abdomen, and even be cautious with kids as they may hit your abdomen and don't lift them.

Week 15:

Baby Development: Facial features are taking shape.

Baby Size: As big as a pear.

Tips: Maintain oral hygiene, eat snacks before exercise, and learn about preeclampsia and baby's fundal height. Go for an Amniocentesis(test done to check any chromosomal abnormalities)

Week 16:

Baby Development: The baby can hear, and the intestines and muscles are growing stronger.

Baby Size: As big as an avocado.

Tips: Try yoga for back pain, eat leafy vegetables, and prepare for the quad screen.

Week 17:

Baby Development: Rapid growth continues; early symptoms subside. But you start to eat more and more, don't worry as your baby is getting bigger and hungrier.

Sciatica is a nerve, the largest in the body starts in the lower back, runs down the buttocks, and branches down at the back of the legs to ankles and feet, sharp shooting pain, tingling, or numbness that starts in the back or buttocks and radiates down the legs happens when a nerve gets compressed by bulging, slipped or ruptured discs. Try a heating pad or back stretches to ease the pain.

To relieve round ligament pain make sure to spend time off your feet and decrease the intensity of your workouts. You can also consider wearing a belly band for a little extra support.

Baby Size: As big as a large onion.

Tips: avoid sun exposure and cosmetics.

Week 18:

Baby Development: Movements start; ligaments loosen due to relaxin hormone.

Baby Size: As big as a cucumber.

Tips: don't make any sudden moves, be careful while getting up, especially after lying down, turn to the side, and slowly lift yourself.

Take iron and calcium-rich foods. Spend at least two hours a day speaking with your child and pampering your womb. This creates a bond between you both. And also imagine how you want your baby to be physically, mentally, and behaviour-wise.

Week 19:

Baby Development: Tiny kicks become noticeable; now your halfway through pregnancy.

Baby Size: As big as a mango.

Tips: Increase fiber intake and drink plenty of fluids.

Week 20:

Baby Development: Lungs are developing.

Baby Size: As big as a sweet potato.

Tips: Include iron-rich foods and. Have nuts and dry fruits as they are full of Vitamin E, proteins, and important minerals. Though they are rich in fat but are good for baby-brain boosting DHA.

Week 21:

Baby Development: Limb control improves, and now Your baby swallows a bit of amniotic fluid each day, not only for nutrition and hydration but also to practice swallowing and digestion skills. And keep this in mind- the taste of the amniotic fluid differs from day to day depending on what you've eaten- spicy food one day, sweet dish the next. The variety of flavours won't confuse your baby since your little one has very developed taste buds already. Researchers have noted that babies who were exposed to certain tastes in utero via the amniotic fluid were more eager to eat foods with those same tastes after birth.

Baby Size: As big as a large banana.

Tips: Elevate your feet, avoid hair removal creams, and focus on gradual weight gain.

Week 22:

Baby Development: Grip, vision, and hearing strengthens. Braxton Hicks contractions (you feel irregular painless, squeezing sensations in your abdomen), these are also called false labour pain.

Baby Size: As big as a papaya.

Tips: Practice yoga, consider a fibronectin test, and eat magnesium-rich foods.

Week 23:

Baby Development: Fetal activity increases; red palms and feet are common.

Baby Size: As big as a carrot.

Tips: Stay hydrated and try for pilates.

Week 24:

Baby Development: Baby can hear external and internal sounds.

Baby Size: As big as corn.

Tips: Prepare for glucose screening, take shorter showers, and monitor weight gain.

Week 25:

Baby Development: Baby's nose and lungs become functional.

Baby Size: As big as an eggplant.

Tips: Apply moisturizer for itching and talk to a doctor if feeling low or depressed.

Week 26:

Baby Development: Baby's eyes may open; insomnia may increase.

Baby Size: As big as spaghetti squash.

Tips: Limit fluids after 6 pm to reduce nighttime discomfort.

Week 27:

Baby Development: Approaching the third trimester.

Baby Size: As big as a cabbage.

Tips: Monitor your heart rate during workouts.

Third trimester

Week 28:

Baby Development: The baby can now blink and even dream.

Baby Size: As big as a head of lettuce.

Tips: Check your Rh status, ask about breast changes, add iron supplements, skip fish oil supplements, and select a childbirth class.

Week 29:

Baby Development: baby Movement may feel tighter as space becomes limited.

Baby Size: As big as a head of cauliflower.

Tips: Buy breast pads, stay active to prevent Restless Leg Syndrome (RLS), and consider cord blood banking.

Week 30:

Baby Development: Fetal movements, gas, swelling, and breathlessness are common.

Baby Size: As big as a beetroot (including leaves).

Tips- But standing up straight can give your lungs a little well, breathing room. Don't make any sudden moves, be careful while getting up, especially after lying down, turn to the side, and slowly lift yourself. Take iron and calcium-rich foods. Spend at least two hours a day speaking with your child and pampering your womb. This creates a bond between you both. And also imagine how you want your baby to be physically, mentally, and behaviour-wise. Sleep semi-seated on your left side with pillows propping you up.

Week 31:

Baby Development: The baby's brain becomes more sophisticated and active

Baby Size: As big as a coconut.

Tips: Pack your hospital bag, monitor facial swelling, stay hydrated, and wear comfortable shoes.

Week 32:

Baby Development: The baby practices sucking, breathing, and swallowing.

Tips: Learn the signs of early labor and moisturize regularly.

Week 33:

Baby Development: Baby grows rapidly and practices kicking; shortness of breath may intensify.

Tips: Add more calcium to your diet and sleep on your side to maximize blood flow.

Week 34:

Baby Development: The baby weighs around five pounds, like a bag of flour.

Tips: Use salt moderately but don't overdo it.

Week 35:

Baby Development: The baby may shift to a head-down position while building body fat and brain matter.

Tips: Prepare for Braxton Hicks contractions and monitor your body's changes.

Week 36:

Baby Development: Hormones increase joint flexibility as labor approaches.

Tips: Get your labor questions answered, prepare for a GBS test, and plan to track feeding and diaper changes.

Week 37-38:

Baby Development: Lungs are fully developed; the baby is ready for birth.

Baby Size: As big as a mini watermelon.

Tips: Finalize postpartum meal plans, double-check your hospital bag, and sample labor-inducing foods.

Week 39:

Baby Development: Baby is full-term and ready for birth.

Tips: Watch for labor signs, pack light snacks if approved. **Breech baby-** if your baby is in breech position (if your baby is lying bottom or feet first), many nurse-midwives recommend specific exercises you can do to help your baby turn down the best exit strategy when it comes to birthing. Try doing pelvic tilts or kneeling with your knees hip-width apart, bending over so your breasts touch the floor and your belly nearly does, repeat three times a day with the help of someone.

Weeks 40-42:

Baby Development: Baby reaches full-term size (as big as a watermelon).

Tips: Prepare for possible induction with Pitocin, note bowel changes as a sign of labor, and consider an epidural. Stay calm—your baby will arrive soon!

Parenting During Pregnancy

Is it Safe to Use Electronic Gadgets during Pregnancy?

Recent research highlights the potential risks of electronic gadgets due to radioactive and electromagnetic radiation. These risks include potential impacts on fetal development, sleep patterns, and brain function. Here's a summary of findings and preventive measures:

Research Findings:

Cell Phones:

Radiation from cell phones can harm the fetus, especially when the phone is kept too close to the body.

Studies link maternal phone usage during pregnancy to disrupted sleep patterns in children.

Personal Computers (PCs):

PCs emit electromagnetic fields that can negatively impact fetal development when used for prolonged periods.

Sitting for long hours in front of a computer may increase the risk of adverse effects.

Wi-Fi:

Wi-Fi releases low levels of radiation, which can become harmful with extended exposure.

Continuous Wi-Fi use should be minimized.

Laptops and Tablets:

Close proximity to these devices and their tendency to overheat can raise body temperature, posing risks to the fetus.

Overheating may lead to changes in fetal development.

Memory and Brain Development:

Studies, including those on pregnant mice, show potential effects on brain development, memory, and sleep cycles due to prolonged exposure to gadget radiation.

Preventive Measures:

Minimize Use:

Limit screen time and avoid prolonged exposure to gadgets.

Use devices only when necessary.

Take Breaks:

Regular breaks can reduce exposure and improve posture.

Maintain Distance:

Keep gadgets at a safe distance from your body, especially during use.

Turn Off Wi-Fi:

Switch off Wi-Fi when not in use to minimize radiation exposure.

Avoid Overheating:

Avoid placing laptops or tablets directly on your lap. Use a table or stand to maintain distance and prevent overheating.

Bedroom Rules:

Keep electronic devices out of the bedroom to avoid radiation exposure during rest.

Set phones to airplane mode when not in use.

Maintain Proper Posture:

Ensure ergonomic posture to avoid physical strain from prolonged gadget use.

By taking these precautions, you can reduce potential risks associated with electronic gadgets and prioritize the health and development of your baby.

Does Playing Mind Games and Solving Puzzles Good for the Baby during Pregnancy?

Pregnancy is a time of immense change and anticipation, often accompanied by stress. Engaging in relaxing and enjoyable activities can significantly benefit both the mother and the unborn baby. Studies suggest that staying positive, calm, and engaged in productive activities fosters better development for the baby. Here are some games and activities you can try to keep yourself happy and stress-free:

Creative and Relaxing Activities:

Painting:

A therapeutic form of self-expression and meditation.

You don't need to be an artist; try DIY paint kits to create something unique.

Mandala Art:

Known to reduce stress, improve sleep, and ease depression.

DIY mandala art kits are a great starting point.

Candle Making:

A calming and satisfying activity. Use DIY kits to create scented candles for relaxation.

Doodle Art:

Enhances focus, improves concentration, and relieves stress.

Let your creativity flow with simple doodling exercises.

Art and Craft Kits:

Transform your craft ideas into beautiful creations, keeping your mind engaged.

DIY Cushion Making:

Learn sewing skills while making something useful and pretty. A unique and productive stress buster.

Games to Play with Loved Ones:

Telestrations:

A sketch-and-guess game that guarantees laughter and bonding with family.

Pictionary:

Draw and guess phrases in this fun and interactive game, perfect for group enjoyment.

Scrabble:

Improve vocabulary and focus while having fun.

Sagrada:

A dice-placement game that challenges your creativity and strategy skills.

Azul:

A tile-placement game to compete in creating beautiful patterns.

Brain-Boosting Puzzles and Games:

Sudoku:

A number puzzle that enhances logical thinking and focus.

Rubik's Cube:

The world's most famous puzzle that boosts problem-solving skills.

Chess:

Develops strategic thinking, memory, and cognitive abilities.

Jigsaw Puzzles:

Solving large puzzles improves brain activity and provides a satisfying sense of achievement.

Other Beneficial Activities:

Candlelit Meditation: Use your DIY candles to create a serene atmosphere.

Board Games: Bond with your family over simple board games.

Knitting or Crocheting: Create something meaningful while relaxing your mind.

Engaging in these activities not only relieves stress but also nurtures your mental well-being. A happy and calm mother contributes significantly to the baby's healthy development. Choose the activities that resonate with you, and enjoy this special time!

Can Solving of Maths problems and Geometric activity during Pregnancy affect your Baby

Several studies have shown that maternal stress is linked to emotional and behavioural problems in the child. There was a study conducted to observe whether a mother's cognitive ability affects fetal brain blood flow, which influences fetal brain development.

Thirty-five women in the 20th to 40th week of pregnancy were engaged in mathematical activity. Fetal middle cerebral artery, Pulsatility index, and Peak systolic velocity were monitored before, during, and after activity. The results were, that the brain activity of the mother was linked to fetal brain blood flow in the arteries supplying to most brain regions and possibly increased brain activity.

Finally, we can conclude that the mother's engagement in mathematical activities and fetal brain blood flow may lead to the enhancement of the fetus's brain function and cognitive advantage for the child. It has both short and long-term physiological changes, which result in the development of mathematical and other cognitive abilities of children from the womb itself.

Try solving daily some 5-7 math problems, solve tables, and solve small math questions that you used to solve during your school days, it should be a fun activity don't create too much stress. Try addition, subtraction, multiplication, division, and counting. These are enough for your development. Daily engage in this activity for an hour not more than that.

Does Reading Books during Pregnancy Affect Your Child?

Reading books is one of the best hobbies of every successful person. Books are one's best friend. Reading books during pregnancy not only increases knowledge but also strengthens the bond between you and your child. It triggers better concentration, good attention, de stress resulting you a smarter child.

Babies start to hear by the second trimester, they can remember your voice and the stories you read and taught them. Even our Ancestors used to say, read, and listen to the stories of Great Personalities who have achieved success in their lives which inspires your child and gives good values to them. It is said in all cultures and religions.

Try reading some Inspirational, Motivational, and Spiritual books, stories of Great Personalities, and books of moral values. Here are some books that I recommend, you can choose according to your will- Garba Geeta, Ramayana, Krishna Leela, Bhagwat Geeta, Quran, Bible, Shiv Puran, Devi Puran, Stories of Great Personalities, Stories of Tenali Rama, Stories of Birbal, Panchatantra, Rhymes and Poems of Moral values, etc.

Recent studies have found that the environment around the unborn baby that includes,including the mother's thinking including what she sees and hears, the father's behaviour, and surrounding people's behaviour determines the character and interest of your child in the future. Let me give you a real-life example, once a father wished for his unborn child to love football, so he created a similar atmosphere near his wife, by getting footballs, pasting posters of football players, watching, and discussing matches together, and now his son is a football player.So decide wisely what type of child you want and create a similar atmosphere.

How does Music affect your Baby's development during Pregnancy?

Music has a vital role in your child's development, even before birth. Exposing your child to music ignites all areas of child development. And doing this early can help ensure that your baby grows up healthy. Listening to music during pregnancy will not only have a soothing and uplifting effect on the pregnant woman but also a positive influence on the unborn baby.

By 24 weeks of pregnancy, the baby starts to develop hearing and respond to voices and noise outside. An unborn baby can recognise her mother's voice, her native language, word patterns and rhymes.

The English word "Lullaby" is thought to come from the "lala" or "lulu" sounds made by mothers or nurses to calm children. "Bye" is another lulling sound or a term to say "good night". A lullaby, or so-called cradle song, has a story to soothe babies and small children to sleep. But be careful with only calming music, as louder and high-intensity sounds are harmful to your baby. Instrumental music and relaxing and soothing music are good for your baby.

Bonding with your Baby from the Womb

Bonding starts within the womb itself. As your baby is growing from your own body. This stage is perfect to begin your attachment with your baby.

Here are some ways you can have a bond- talk and sing to your baby, gently touch or rub your belly or massage it, and respond to your baby's kicks. In the last trimester, you can gently push against the baby or rub your belly where the kick has occurred and see if there is a response. Play music to your baby such as lullaby or any other soothing music. Talk about your family to your baby. Tell some stories and read books aloud. Think and imagine about your baby. Write down what you feel as a dairy to your child. Spend more time with kids. Discuss with your parents about their parenting journey.

And finally, Prepare yourself for this journey, plan what to do and what not to do not only about giving a comfortable life to them but about your parenting style, what you are going to teach them, what unique would be in your parenting style etc.

And remember, according to me, **"One doesn't become a parent just by giving birth, it's about a feeling, an attachment that prioritises your child over your own identity".**

Happy parenting!!!

Surrogacy – There Bun My Oven!

Surrogacy is an incredible, life-changing experience. Whether you know someone struggling with infertility or simply enjoy the journey of pregnancy but don't wish to expand your own family, surrogacy offers a profound way to help others achieve their dream of parenthood. If you're considering becoming a surrogate, it's important to prepare yourself for both the physical and emotional aspects of this journey.

1. Be Ready for an Emotional Journey

Surrogacy is deeply emotional, and it's essential to prepare yourself for the emotional challenges ahead. You'll be helping someone else create or grow their family, which is a unique and profound experience. However, the emotional aspect of surrogacy goes beyond just helping others. Hormonal changes, physical changes, and the responsibility of carrying someone else's child can stir up a range of emotions. Understanding that you'll be carrying a baby as if it were your own, but with the knowledge that you'll hand them over at the end of the pregnancy, is key to navigating this emotional journey.

2. Ensure Your Body is Ready Physically for Surrogacy

Even though you've experienced pregnancy before, becoming a surrogate comes with its own set of considerations. It's important to ensure your body is physically ready for the demands of surrogacy. This may involve evaluating your overall health, lifestyle, and any potential changes needed to ensure a healthy pregnancy. Whether it's adjusting your diet, exercising, or addressing any underlying health issues, taking the time to assess your readiness will set you up for success. Consider consulting with your healthcare provider to make sure you're in optimal physical condition to carry a baby for someone else.

3. Be in the Right State of Mind

Mental preparation is just as crucial as physical readiness. Surrogacy is a nine-month journey, and it's essential to mentally prepare for the emotional and physical demands that come with it. You will need patience, resilience, and the ability to manage both the highs and lows that may arise throughout the process. It's a commitment that requires focus, so take time to reflect on your reasons for pursuing surrogacy and ensure you're ready to embark on this unique path.

4. Understand the Surrogacy Requirements

Each surrogacy program has specific requirements. These may include age restrictions, health assessments, and lifestyle guidelines. Before moving forward, it's important to review these requirements thoroughly. Many fertility clinics and surrogacy agencies provide detailed guidelines on their websites. Understanding what is required will help you assess if you're eligible and if surrogacy is a viable option for you.

5. Research the Surrogacy Process

The surrogacy process can take anywhere from 14 to 20 months, and it's essential to educate yourself on the entire journey. From your initial application and medical screenings to matching with intended parents and the eventual embryo transfer, there are many milestones along the way. Understanding the general timeline of the process will help you manage expectations and plan accordingly. Thanks to online resources, there's now a wealth of information available to help you understand what's involved in the surrogacy process, so take the time to do your research.

6. Share Your Decision with Family and Friends

One of the most important steps before starting your surrogacy journey is sharing your decision with your loved ones. Surrogacy can be a complex and emotional process, and having the support of your family and friends will be invaluable. Open communication will ensure that everyone is on the same page, and it will allow your loved ones to be there for you throughout your journey. Their support can make all the difference when you face challenges during the process.

7. Understand the Time Commitment

Surrogacy is a significant time commitment. From medical appointments to the eventual delivery, the entire process will take up a considerable portion of your life. It's essential to assess how surrogacy will fit into your existing responsibilities and whether you can fully dedicate yourself to the journey. Take time to reflect on your schedule, family obligations, and personal life to ensure that you're able to make this commitment.

8. Connect with Experienced Surrogates

Reading about surrogacy is helpful, but nothing compares to hearing firsthand experiences from those who have already gone through the process. Connecting with experienced surrogates will give you valuable insights into what the journey is truly like. Having open, honest conversations with other surrogates will help you better understand the challenges, rewards, and everything in between. Their advice can help you navigate the process with more confidence and clarity.

9. Build an Open, Trusting Relationship with Your Intended Parents

Surrogacy is a partnership between you and the intended parents. It's important to approach this relationship with openness and trust. Communication is key throughout the process, as it helps foster a strong bond between you and the parents you're helping. You may share important milestones and moments along the way, so developing a good rapport will ensure a positive experience for everyone involved. Establishing clear expectations and staying in regular contact will help you maintain a strong, supportive relationship with your intended parents.

By preparing yourself mentally, physically, and emotionally, you can embark on this incredible journey with confidence and a sense of fulfillment. Surrogacy is a gift—one that will have a lasting impact on the lives of others and on your own.

ADOPTION

The Joy and Preparation of Bringing a Child Into Your Life

There's no feeling more exhilarating than welcoming a child into your home for the first time. Whether the child is joining your family through natural birth or adoption, the experience is truly indescribable. The journey of parenthood brings a unique sense of fulfillment and joy, but it also comes with its own set of responsibilities. To ensure a smooth transition into this new chapter, it's important to be well-prepared in various aspects of your life. There are four primary categories to consider when preparing for the arrival of your child:

1. Basic Needs: Creating a Safe and Nurturing Environment

Every child has fundamental needs that must be met for their well-being and development. These include:

Unconditional Love: A child's emotional and psychological development relies heavily on love and affection. As a parent, providing a loving and supportive environment will help them feel secure and valued.

Shelter: A safe, comfortable home is essential for your child's sense of stability. Make sure your living space is child-friendly and conducive to their growth.

Clothing: Ensure that you have a variety of appropriate clothing for your child, from daily wear to seasonal needs.

Food and Nutrition: Proper nutrition is vital for a child's growth and health. Plan for feeding supplies and healthy meals, whether you are breastfeeding or formula-feeding.

Medical Care: Regular check-ups and access to healthcare are crucial to monitor your child's physical health and development.

Fun Activities: Providing toys, books, and opportunities for play helps foster your child's cognitive and emotional growth. It's essential to have a variety of stimulating activities that engage their curiosity and creativity.

One of the first steps is to prepare a designated room for your child, whether it's a nursery or shared space. A crib or bed, changing table, clothing storage, and shelves for books and toys are important components of the setup.

2. Financial Needs: Planning for the Future

Adoption or the arrival of a child is not just an emotional investment; it's also a financial one. Raising a child involves ongoing expenses that require careful planning and budgeting. Here are a few things to keep in mind:

Adoption Costs: If you're adopting, it's important to understand the financial costs involved, including legal fees, agency fees, and any other related expenses. These can vary depending on the type of adoption, but it's essential to budget for them.

Childcare and Education: As your child grows, you'll need to consider costs related to childcare, education, and extracurricular activities. These expenses can increase over time, so it's important to plan ahead.

Emergency Savings: Building a financial cushion for emergencies is crucial before bringing your child home. Unexpected expenses can arise, and having a nest egg will provide peace of mind during challenging times.

Ongoing Expenses: From diapers and baby supplies to medical costs and beyond, the ongoing costs of raising a child are significant. Having a stable income and financial strategy will help you manage these expenses with ease.

Creating a detailed budget and financial plan before your child's arrival will set you up for success and ensure you are prepared for the financial demands of parenthood.

3. Emotional Needs: Preparing to Be a Loving and Supportive Parent

While the physical and financial preparations are important, the emotional aspect of parenting is just as crucial. Preparing to meet the emotional needs of a new child requires self-reflection, empathy, and patience. Here's how you can get ready:

Providing Emotional Stability: Your child will look to you for emotional guidance, security, and comfort. It's essential to create a safe, nurturing environment where they feel loved and supported at all times.

Patience and Flexibility: Parenting is a journey filled with both rewarding and challenging moments. Be prepared for sleepless nights, difficult transitions, and the emotional ups and downs that come with raising a child. Patience is key, and understanding that both you and your child will grow and adapt together will help you navigate the journey.

Open Communication: Whether your child is an infant or an older child, maintaining open communication is essential. As your child grows, they will need to feel heard and understood. Be ready to listen to their needs and provide guidance and support as they express their feelings and emotions.

Creating a Bond: Whether through adoption or birth, forming a strong emotional bond with your child is one of the most fulfilling parts of parenting. Take time to engage with your child, share experiences, and build a deep, lasting connection. This bond will form the foundation of their emotional well-being.

As a parent, your emotional preparedness will play a significant role in helping your child feel secure, loved, and understood. Be prepared to provide them with the support they need to thrive emotionally.

4. Social and Community Needs: Building a Support System

The journey of parenthood is not one you have to face alone. Surrounding yourself with a strong support system is vital for both you and your child. Consider these elements:

Family and Friends: Having a network of loved ones to lean on will provide you with emotional support, advice, and assistance when needed. Whether it's help with childcare, offering words of encouragement, or just being there for a listening ear, family and friends are invaluable.

Parenting Groups: Joining parenting groups or online communities can provide support and connection with other parents. Sharing experiences and learning from others who are on a similar journey can be incredibly helpful.

Professional Support: It's also important to seek professional guidance if needed, whether through counseling, paediatric care, or parenting classes. Don't hesitate to reach out for expert advice on child development, health concerns, or emotional well-being.

A well-rounded support system can make all the difference in your journey to parenthood, offering both practical assistance and emotional strength as you navigate the challenges and joys of raising a child.

Bringing a child into your life, whether through adoption or birth, is one of the most rewarding experiences you can have. By addressing the basic needs, financial planning, emotional preparation, and support systems before your child arrives, you can ensure that both you and your new family member are ready for this incredible adventure. Parenting is a lifelong journey filled with learning, growth, and endless love—making sure you're well-prepared will help you embrace it with confidence and joy.

Single Parent

The Reality and Beauty of Single Parenthood

There's no denying that being a single parent comes with its own set of challenges. The journey of parenthood is never easy, regardless of whether you're raising a child alone or with a partner. But when you're a single parent, the responsibility is magnified. You are both the mother and the father, juggling countless tasks and decisions every single day. In addition to the daily demands of parenting, single parents often cope with feelings of loneliness, stress, and self-doubt.

It's important to recognize that single parents may face judgment or misunderstandings from others. People may criticize your relationship status or downplay the difficulties you face, without fully grasping the emotional and practical weight of your situation. But amidst these struggles, there are many positive aspects of single parenthood that are worth celebrating.

1. Freedom and Independence: Embracing the Autonomy

One of the advantages of single parenthood is the freedom to make decisions independently. As a single parent, you have the ability to shape your family's routine and lifestyle without having to compromise with a partner. This freedom allows you to set the pace for your family's day-to-day life, from meal planning to family activities, and even financial decisions. You get to decide what works best for you and your child without needing to consider the opinions or preferences of someone else.

While this can feel overwhelming at times, it can also provide a sense of control and empowerment. Single parents have the opportunity to create a household that aligns with their own values, routines, and goals, without needing to negotiate or compromise.

2. Personal Growth and Self-Discovery: A Path to Strength

Being a single parent often requires immense personal growth. You are tasked with managing everything on your own, which forces you to become resourceful, adaptable, and resilient. You learn to balance work, household chores, and parenting responsibilities, all while managing your own emotions and needs.

The journey of single parenthood can help you discover strengths you may not have known you had. Over time, you develop a deeper understanding of your own abilities, strengths, and limits. It teaches you to be more patient, more organized, and more compassionate— qualities that serve you well in all aspects of life.

Additionally, the experience can lead to greater self-reliance and confidence. As you face challenges head-on and overcome obstacles, you grow not only as a parent but as an individual.

This personal growth can enrich your relationships with others and help you build a stronger sense of self-worth.

3. Building a Unique Bond with Your Children: Strengthening the Connection

One of the most beautiful aspects of single parenthood is the deep and unique bond you can form with your children. Without a second parent in the home, you often become your child's primary source of support, comfort, and guidance. This can lead to an incredibly strong emotional connection between you and your child, built on mutual trust and reliance.

As a single parent, you have the opportunity to be the sole influence in shaping your child's upbringing, which can lead to a profound and intimate relationship. You're able to instill your values, beliefs, and perspectives in a way that is personal and direct.

Moreover, this bond often leads to a greater understanding of each other's needs and emotions. Single parents often become more attuned to their child's feelings and desires, which can foster open communication and a deep sense of connection. This relationship can also teach your child the importance of resilience, love, and the power of family.

4. Developing a Support Network: The Importance of Community

While single parenthood can be isolating at times, it also encourages the development of a strong support system. Many single parents learn to rely on friends, family members, and other parents for emotional and practical support. This network can be a lifeline, providing encouragement, help with childcare, and advice when needed.

By surrounding yourself with a community that understands your challenges, you can alleviate some of the loneliness and stress that comes with single parenting. In turn, this network of support can also help you stay connected to your own needs and desires, ensuring that you don't lose sight of your own well-being.

5. Cherishing the Gift of Parenthood

Ultimately, parenthood—whether as a single parent or not—is a beautiful and life-changing experience. The love you share with your child, the milestones you witness, and the joy that comes from watching them grow are all priceless gifts.

Single parents often learn to appreciate the small moments and victories in ways that others might take for granted. Each day presents an opportunity to create memories, overcome challenges, and build a legacy of love and care.

Despite the difficulties, the experience of being a single parent can be one of the most rewarding of your life. It's a journey that requires patience, sacrifice, and determination, but it's also filled with profound moments of joy, love, and fulfillment. No matter the circumstances, the bond you share with your child is irreplaceable and worth cherishing.

In conclusion, while single parenthood comes with its fair share of challenges, it also offers opportunities for growth, independence, and deep connection. Embracing the journey of single parenting with a positive mindset and a supportive community can make the experience incredibly rewarding. Parenthood is a gift, and being a single parent can be a beautiful expression of love, strength, and resilience.

Guardian

Understanding Guardianship and the Qualities of a Good Guardian

A guardian is an individual who takes on the responsibility of caring for another person, ensuring their well-being, and making legal decisions on their behalf. Guardianship often extends to managing the individual's property and safeguarding their interests. For children, a guardian steps in as a parental figure, offering stability and guidance, particularly in situations where parents are unable to fulfill their role. Choosing the right guardian is a critical decision, as this person will have a profound impact on the child's physical, emotional, and financial well-being.

To ensure the child thrives under their care, a good guardian should possess certain key qualities. These traits help create a nurturing environment that promotes growth, stability, and resilience during challenging times.

Essential Qualities of a Good Guardian

1. Patience: A Pillar of Understanding

Raising children requires immense patience, as every parent knows. Children often test boundaries, act out, and need guidance to navigate their emotions and behaviors. When the child is dealing with the trauma of losing their parents or adapting to a new guardian, patience becomes even more crucial.

A guardian who is naturally calm and composed is more likely to approach difficult situations with understanding rather than frustration. They should be prepared to handle tantrums, misbehavior, and emotional outbursts with a steady hand. Their ability to remain patient fosters a sense of security in the child, helping them feel valued and understood as they process their emotions.

2. Empathy and Kindness: Foundations of Emotional Support

Empathy is the ability to understand and share another person's feelings, while kindness is the expression of care and compassion toward others. Together, these qualities are essential for a guardian, especially when dealing with children who have faced significant life changes.

Children need more than just physical care; they require emotional support to feel secure and loved. A guardian who can empathize with a child's struggles—be it grief, fear, or confusion—creates a safe space for the child to express their feelings. This emotional understanding, paired with acts of kindness, helps the child build trust and confidence in their new environment.

Empathy and kindness also teach children how to approach the world with compassion, which is a valuable life lesson that will shape their character as they grow.

3. Financial Stability: A Cornerstone of Practical Care

Financial stability is one of the most critical qualities of a good guardian. Caring for a child involves ongoing expenses, from basic necessities like food and clothing to education, healthcare, and extracurricular activities.

A guardian who is already struggling financially may find it challenging to manage the added responsibility of raising a child. It's important to choose someone who has the financial means to provide a stable and secure environment. This doesn't mean they need to be wealthy, but they should have a steady income, a good understanding of budgeting, and the ability to manage resources effectively.

Financial stability ensures that the child's needs are met without unnecessary stress or compromises, allowing them to grow up in a supportive and secure environment.

4. Parenting Style: Aligning Values and Approaches

Every parent has their own unique parenting style, shaped by their experiences, values, and beliefs. When selecting a guardian, it's important to consider how their approach to parenting aligns with your own values and the needs of your child.

For potential guardians who are already parents, observing how they interact with their children can provide valuable insight into their parenting style. Do they prioritize discipline or encouragement? Are they hands-on and involved, or more laid-back? Understanding these nuances will help you determine if their style aligns with your vision for your child's upbringing.

For those who don't have children of their own, it's essential to evaluate their interactions with your child or other children. Their ability to connect, communicate, and set boundaries can give you an idea of how they might step into the role of a guardian.

Additional Considerations When Choosing a Guardian

Beyond these qualities, there are other factors to consider:

Emotional Connection: A strong bond between the child and the guardian can ease the transition and provide a sense of familiarity.

Proximity and Availability: A guardian who lives nearby or is willing to relocate may make the transition smoother and allow the child to maintain existing routines and relationships.

Health and Energy: A guardian should have the physical and emotional capacity to care for a child, especially if the child has specific needs or requires extra attention.

Values and Beliefs: Ensure that the guardian's values align with yours, especially regarding education, religion, and life goals.

Being a guardian is a profound responsibility that requires a blend of patience, empathy, financial stability, and thoughtful parenting.

It's not just about providing a home; it's about creating a nurturing environment where a child can heal, grow, and thrive.

When choosing a guardian, it's essential to consider not only their practical abilities but also their emotional readiness and commitment to the child's well-being. A good guardian doesn't have to be perfect—they just need to be willing to offer their love, time, and effort to ensure the child feels supported and cared for in every way.

Ultimately, guardianship is an act of love, a testament to the enduring bond between family and friends, and a commitment to ensuring a child's future is bright and secure.

Breast-feeding and Post-partum recovery (after childbirth):

Breastfeeding (chest feeding) is a natural way to feed your baby. In this method of feeding your baby, they latch on or attach their mouth onto your breast and, through a sucking motion, drink milk made by your body. Your baby will likely start breastfeeding not long after they're born, often within the first few hours.

At first, your milk supply will be made up of something called colostrum. This is a protein-rich, often thick liquid that helps your baby stay hydrated. It's full of antibodies that also help guard your newborn against infections. Your colostrum will change into mature milk after the first few days (usually three to five days) of breastfeeding. During this time your baby will lose a bit of weight. This is normal. They will regain it once your milk "comes in".

There are many natural benefits of breastfeeding that both you and your baby can enjoy. Your breast milk is not only a nutritious choice for your baby, it also can help protect them from certain illnesses. When you're sick, your body creates antibodies. These antibodies are passed from you to your baby through your breast milk. This helps protect your baby. Breastfed babies have a lower risk for developing certain medical conditions, including: Diabetes,Obesity,Asthma and Ear infections.

Breastfed infants also have a lower risk of sudden infant death syndrome (SIDS). New parents can benefit from breastfeeding (chest feeding) too. Many nursing parents say that breastfeeding helped them get back to their pre-pregnancy weight faster. It can also help you with blood pressure issues, reduce your risk of developing Type 2 diabetes, and even reduce your risk of breast and ovarian cancer.

Breastfeeding can actually start in the hour's right after your baby is born. After your baby is born, you might be encouraged to hold your baby against your skin – called skin-to-skin contact. This close contact encourages your baby to bond and breastfeed.

Once you're ready, place your baby to your breast in a position that's comfortable for both of you. Guide your baby's mouth to your nipple. When your baby is properly latched on your breast, their mouth should cover most of your areola (the darker area that encircles your nipple). Typically, you'll feel your baby pull on your nipple as they feed. You might hear small noises as your baby eats. Breastfeeding shouldn't be painful. If it is, your baby might not be latched on to your breast correctly.

There is a learning curve to breastfeeding. You will need to try different holds with your baby and learn what works best for both of you. You'll also need to learn your baby's schedule. This can vary depending on each child. It's important to not be too attached to a schedule — your baby will make their own schedule and you will adapt to it over time. There's no set amount of times your baby will eat each day. Feed your baby when they are hungry. For many babies, this is every two to three hours.

A part of early breastfeeding also involves learning your baby's cues. Your baby will do certain things when he or she is hungry. **Cues of hunger can include:**

Sucking on their hands.

Acting alert.

Moving towards your breast.

Once a baby starts crying, it might be a late stage of hunger. Try to feed your baby before they start to cry. Once your baby starts crying, it might be harder to get them to feed properly.

Breastfeeding is a learned skill and takes practice, but the health benefits you gain for you and your baby are worth it. Help with breastfeeding is available. There are many ways for you to learn about breastfeeding. Many hospitals offer breastfeeding classes that you can attend during pregnancy. In most cases, nurses and lactation consultants are also available to give you information and support. Talking to other breastfeeding people might be helpful and make you feel more comfortable.

you don't have to drink milk to make breast milk. Other sources of calcium-rich foods include yogurt, cheese, tofu, salmon, almonds, calcium-enriched fruit juice, leafy green vegetables, broccoli, and dried beans and peas. Eat four servings of calcium-rich foods every day to provide proper nutrition for you and your baby. You can also ask your provider about calcium and vitamin D supplements.

Similarly to when you were pregnant, you should pay attention to what you eat and drink when you're breastfeeding. There aren't as many restrictions when you're breastfeeding as there are when you are pregnant, but a few things to keep in mind include:

Cutting back on your caffeine. You can drink caffeine when you're breastfeeding, but try to limit it to about 200 milligrams each day. You might also want to time your cup of coffee so that you're not drinking caffeine before your child's nap or bedtime feeding. The caffeine could pass through your milk and to your baby.

Limiting your alcohol intake. You can also drink a limited amount of alcohol when you're breastfeeding. However, you should wait a few hours (at least two) after a drink before you feed your baby. Over time, the alcohol will leave your system. It's safest for your baby if you wait after drinking to breastfeed because it can pass through your milk and could possibly cause harm.

It's also good to quit smoking if you haven't already. Secondhand smoke is dangerous to children. Smoking is not only harmful to your children and your own health, but it can also decrease your milk supply. You shouldn't smoke — or use any other type of drug — around your baby.

If you're shy, there are several ways you can still breastfeed and feel comfortable. You can choose to feed your baby in private. Or, you can breastfeed in front of others without them seeing anything. You can wear shirts that pull up from the bottom, just enough for your baby to reach your breast. You can put a blanket over your shoulder or around your baby so no one can see your breast.

If you can take your baby with you, your baby can eat when they are hungry. If you need to be away from your baby, you can pump or "express" your milk and refrigerate it so that someone else can feed your baby from a bottle.

When you return to work, you can learn to pump or "express" your milk and refrigerate or freeze it so that someone else can feed your milk to your baby while you're at work. Often, your place of work will have a private space set aside for you to pump.

Some moms find that the following positions are helpful ways to get comfortable and support their babies while breastfeeding. You can also use pillows under your arms, elbows, neck, or back to give you added comfort and support. Keep trying different positions until you are comfortable. What works for one feeding may not work for the next feeding.

Clutch or "football" hold: useful if you had a C-section, or if you have large breasts, flat or inverted nipples, or a strong let-down reflex. This hold is also helpful for babies who like to be in a more upright position when they feed. Hold your baby at your side with the baby lying on his or her back and with his or her head at the level of your nipple. Support your baby's head by placing the palm of your hand at the base of his or her head.

Cross-cradle or transitional hold: useful for premature babies or babies with a weak suck because this hold gives extra head support and may help the baby stay latched. Hold your baby along the area opposite from the breast you are using. Support your baby's head at the base of his or her neck with the palm of your hand.

Cradle hold: an easy, common hold that is comfortable for most mothers and babies. Hold your baby with his or her head on your forearm and his or her body facing yours.

Laid-back hold (straddle hold): a more relaxed, baby-led approach. Lie back on a pillow. Lay your baby against your body with your baby's head just above and between your breasts. Gravity and an instinct to nurse will guide your baby to your breast. As your baby searches for your breast, support your baby's head and shoulders but don't force the latch.

Side-lying position: useful if you had a C-section, but also allows you to rest while the baby breastfeeds. Lie on your side with your baby facing you. Pull your baby close so your baby faces your body.

Below are some common latch problems and how to deal with them.

You're in pain. Many moms say their breasts feel tender when they first start breastfeeding. A mother and her baby need time to find comfortable breastfeeding positions and a good latch. If breastfeeding hurts, your baby may be sucking on only the nipple, and not also on the areola (the darker skin around the nipple).

Gently break your baby's suction to your breast by placing a clean finger in the corner of your baby's mouth. Then try again to get your baby to latch on. To find out if your baby is sucking only on your nipple, check what your nipple looks like when it comes out of your baby's mouth. Your nipple should not look flat or compressed. It should look round and long or the same shape as it was before the feeding.

You or your baby feels frustrated. Take a short break and hold your baby in an upright position. Try holding your baby between your breasts with your skin touching his or her skin (called skin-to-skin). Talk or sing to your baby, or give your baby one of your fingers to suck on for comfort. Try to breastfeed again in a little while.

Your baby has a weak suck or makes tiny sucking movements. Your baby may not have a deep enough latch to suck the milk from your breast. Gently break your baby's suction to your breast by placing a clean finger in the corner of your baby's mouth. Then try to get your baby to latch on again. Talk with a lactation consultant or paediatrician if you are not sure if your baby is getting enough milk. But don't worry. A weak suck is rarely caused by a health problem.

Your baby may be tongue-tied. Babies with a tight or short lingual fraenulum (the piece of tissue attaching the tongue to the floor of the mouth) are described as "tongue-tied." The medical term is ankyloglossia. These babies often find it hard to nurse. They may be unable to extend their tongue past their lower gum line or properly cup the breast during a feed. This can cause slow weight gain in the baby and nipple pain in the mother. If you think your baby may be tongue-tied, talk to your doctor.

Some health problems can make it harder for babies to breastfeed. But breastmilk provides the healthy start your baby needs, which is even more important if your baby is premature or sick. Even if your baby cannot breastfeed directly from you, you can hand express or pump your milk and give it to your baby with a dropper, spoon, or cup, or bottle as your baby gets older.

Some breastfed babies develop jaundice when they do not get enough breastmilk, either because of breastfeeding challenges or because the mother's milk hasn't come in. Jaundice is caused by an excess of bilirubin, which is found in the blood but usually only in very small amounts. In the newborn period, bilirubin can build up faster than it can be removed from the intestinal tract. Jaundice can appear as a yellowing of the skin and eyes. The jaundice usually clears up by 2 weeks of age and usually is not harmful. This type of jaundice usually clears up quickly by breastfeeding more often or feeding of expressed breastmilk or after the mother's milk comes in.Your baby's doctor may monitor his or her bilirubin level with blood tests. Some babies with jaundice may need treatment with a special light (called phototherapy). This light helps break down bilirubin into a form that can be removed from the body easily.Breastfeeding is best for your baby. Even if your baby gets jaundice, this is not something that you caused. Your doctor can help you make sure that your baby is eating well and that the jaundice goes away.

Some babies develop gastroesophageal reflux disease (GERD). GERD happens when the muscle at the opening of the stomach opens at the wrong times. This allows milk and food to come back up into the esophagus, the tube in the throat.

Some symptoms of GERD include:

Severe spitting up or spitting up after every feeding or hours after eating

Projectile vomiting, where the milk shoots out of the mouth

Inconsolable crying, as if in discomfort

Arching of the back, as if in severe pain

Refusal to eat or pulling away from the breast during feeding

Waking up often at night

Slow weight gain

Gagging or choking or having problems swallowing

Many healthy babies might have some of these symptoms and not have GERD. Also, some babies with only a few of these symptoms have a severe case of GERD. Not all babies with GERD spit up or vomit. GERD may need to be treated with medicine if the baby refuses to nurse, gains only a small amount of weight or is losing weight, or has periods of gagging or choking.See your baby's doctor if your baby spits up after every feeding and has any of the other symptoms listed in this section. If your baby has GERD, continue breastfeeding. Infant formula is harder to digest than breastmilk.

Premature birth (also called preterm birth) is when a baby is born before 37 weeks. Premature babies often have a low birth weight (less than 5½ pounds). Both of these can make it challenging to breastfeed, especially if the baby has to stay in the hospital for extra care. But breastmilk helps premature babies grow and stay healthy. Some babies can breastfeed right away. This may be true if your baby was born at a low birth weight but after 37 weeks. These babies will need more skin-to-skin contact to help keep warm. These smaller babies may also need to be fed more often because their stomachs are smaller, and they may get sleepier during those feedings.

If your baby is born prematurely and you are not able to breastfeed at first, you can:Hand express or pump colostrum in the hospital as soon as you are able, Pump milk as often as you would normally breastfeed — about eight times in a 24-hour period (every 3 hours). Give your baby skin-to-skin contact once your baby is ready to breastfeed directly. This can be very calming and a great start to your first feeding. Be sure to work with a lactation consultant on proper latch and positioning. It may take some time for you and your baby to get into a good routine.

Many infants are fussy in the evenings, but if the crying does not stop and gets worse throughout the day or night, it may be caused by colic. Colic usually starts between 2 and 4 weeks of age. A baby may cry inconsolably or scream, extend or pull up his or her legs, and pass gas. The baby's stomach may be enlarged. Crying can happen at any time, although it often gets worse in the early evening.

Colic will probably get better or disappear by the age of 3 or 4 months. Doctors don't know why some babies get colic. Some breastfed babies may be sensitive to certain foods their mother eats, like caffeine, chocolate, dairy, or nuts. Colic could be a sign of a medical problem, such as a hernia or some type of illness. If your infant shows signs of colic, talk to your doctor. Sometimes changing what you eat can help. Some infants seem to be soothed by being held, "worn" with a baby wrap or sling, rocked, or swaddled (wrapped snugly in a blanket). Another tip is to apply a solution of asafoetida(hing) on your baby's navel but nowadays we have roll-on also try it.

Burping your baby is a key part of your baby's feeding routine. When your baby swallows, air bubbles can become trapped in the stomach and cause discomfort. Burping allows your baby to remove some of that gassiness to relieve the pain. It also helps prevent spitting up.

 Signs of trapped gas- Crying, arched back, drawing legs into the tummy or clenching the fists.

 There are no rules on when to burp your baby. Some babies need to be burped during their feed while others after. And some may find it easier than others.

Here are 3 techniques that many parents use. Try them all out to see what works best or use a combination.

Over the shoulder-Hold your baby upright with the head resting on your shoulder. Pat the back with your other hand.

Tip: Cupping your hand slightly is gentler than a flattened palm.

Sitting on your lap- Sit your baby on your lap supporting the chin and chest with one hand. Rub or pat the back with your other hand.

Tip: Use repeated, gentle pats on your baby's back.

Lying across your lap-Rest your baby faced down on your lap and gently rub or pat the back.

Tip: Keep a cloth nearby in case your baby spits up.

If Still showing signs of trapped gas. Try lying your baby on the back and gently massage the tummy. Try moving your baby's legs back and forth, like riding a bike. If these tips don't work, talk to your healthcare provider to advise on alternative options.

Postpartum (or postnatal) refers to the period after childbirth. Most often, the postpartum period is the first six to eight weeks after delivery, or until your body returns to its pre-pregnancy state. But the symptoms and changes that occur during the postpartum period can last far beyond eight weeks.

Major body and life changes are happening at the same time during the postpartum period. Some changes are physical — for example, breast engorgement and vaginal bleeding. Other changes occur due to changing hormones. The bottom line is, giving birth is a major physical and emotional challenge. Being a caregiver and adjusting to life with an infant during the postpartum period is also incredibly demanding.

Pay attention to how you feel after giving birth and let your healthcare provider know if something feels off. Just because you gave birth doesn't mean you're care ends or that your health isn't important. You should try prioritizing resting and taking care of your health in addition to caring for your baby.

Your healthcare provider will schedule postpartum checkups with you so they can continue to monitor your recovery and healing. It's important to attend these appointments because this is where your provider can identify potential complications. This is also a time when you can ask questions and have honest conversations about your healing.

Postpartum recovery timeline. Your recovery — like your pregnancy — is unique to you. There isn't a one-size-fits-all timeline to postpartum. But there's a general timeline of what you can expect. **Some of the things you can expect in the hours and days immediately after birth are:**

Your uterus needs to shrink back to its usual size. This causes cramps and vaginal bleeding. Your provider may even massage your uterus through your belly to help it get smaller.

Hormonal shifts. This can cause symptoms like hot flashes, changes to your mood and headaches.

Breast engorgement. Your breasts will produce milk, and even if you choose not to breastfeed (chest feed), you'll have painful and swollen breasts.

Perineal soreness. It's normal to have pain in the space between your vagina and anus (butthole) if you gave birth vaginally. Up to 70% of people have some degree of vaginal tearing during childbirth. People who have a C-section will feel extra sore around the incision site for a few days.

Swelling from extra fluids. This is typically normal and your body's way of getting rid of fluid you accumulate during pregnancy. Your swelling should go down within a week. When swelling comes with symptoms like chest pain and trouble breathing, it could be a sign of something more serious.

Fatigue. Labor, childbirth and caring for a newborn may introduce you to a new level of exhaustion. Feeling tired for the days and weeks after you give birth is very normal. Trying to rest as much as you can whenever possible will help you feel better.

Physical symptoms in postpartum affect your body — things like what it does, what it looks like and how it feels. **Some of the most common physical symptoms in postpartum are:**

Soreness and pain in your perineum: Your perineum is the space between your vagina and anus. This area stretches, and sometimes tears, during vaginal childbirth. Your entire perineal area may be sore, swollen and tender for weeks after childbirth. Sitting on a pillow, squirting warm water to rinse the area and using a cold sanitary pad are ways to help with this discomfort.

Vaginal discharge: Lochia is the name for the vaginal bleeding you'll have after giving birth (even if you had a C-section). It begins red and tapers off to brown before it ends as a light brown discharge. This entire process can last up to six weeks. Remember, wear a pad to catch vaginal bleeding after childbirth (no tampons).

Uterus involution: This is the medical term for your uterus shrinking back to its pre-pregnancy size. The entire process can take up to six weeks, but it begins almost immediately after your baby is born. You can also expect to feel afterbirth pains (or strong cramps) while this happens. Most of the intense pains go away after a few days, but they can also feel more intense during breastfeeding.

Breast engorgement and nipple pain: You can expect swollen and painful breasts for at least a few days or longer (if you breastfeed). Some people need the help of a lactation consultant to help with painful symptoms of breastfeeding like cracked nipples.

Sweating: Your hormones shift dramatically almost immediately after you give birth. It's common to sweat more, especially at night. It's a normal symptom that should subside within a week or two.

Constipation: Being unable to poop after childbirth is a normal symptom in the postpartum period. If you had an epidural, this can slow down your bowels and make it harder to poop. Sometimes, the fear of pushing to poop leads to constipation. Some healthcare providers recommend stool softeners after you give birth to help. Hemorrhoids are also common in the postpartum period.

C-section recovery: If you have stitches due to a C-section, your skin will take up to 10 days to heal. The deeper stitches can take up to 12 weeks to heal completely. Watch for signs of infection like pus seeping from the incision or having a fever.

Hair loss: Losing your hair is a common occurrence in the postpartum period, mostly due to hormones.

Emotional symptoms in the weeks and months after childbirth involve anything that affects your mind, your stress level or your body image.

Baby blues: Baby blues is feeling sad and teary after giving birth. While these new feelings can take you by surprise, they tend to go away after a few weeks.

Postpartum depression: This is a type of depression that causes extreme sadness and despair in the weeks and months after childbirth. Unlike the baby blues, this doesn't go away and often involves treatment with medication or behavioral therapy.

Postpartum anxiety: Excessive worrying that occurs after having a baby is called postpartum anxiety. It can be accompanied by physical symptoms like losing sleep or heart palpitations. Postpartum depression and postpartum anxiety can often come together. Treatment for postpartum anxiety can also involve medication or behavioral therapy.

Weight loss: Your body went through lots of changes during pregnancy and childbirth. It's common to have loose skin and stretch marks, and stress about extra weight around your hips or belly. Try to relax and give yourself time to recover. You'll lose between 10 and 20 pounds before you leave the hospital. Focus on eating nutritious foods and taking care of yourself. Remember that your body has just been through a lot.

The best thing you can do for your health after you give birth is listen to your body. If something doesn't feel right, please reach out to your healthcare provider. You don't have to wait until your postpartum checkups to call your pregnancy care provider with questions or concerns. Your recovery and overall health are important to them.

One of the most important things you can do for yourself after giving birth is to allow yourself time to rest and heal. While this may be easier said than done, getting rest allows your body and mind time to recover. Ask for help when you need it. This could mean limiting visitors, asking for help with childcare or asking for help with things like cleaning and making meals. **Other than resting, some of the other ways to take care of yourself in the weeks after delivery could involve:**

Nutrition: Try to drink lots of water and eat healthy foods like lean protein, fruit, vegetables and whole grains. Staying hydrated can also help with constipation.

Caring for your perineal area: If you had a vaginal delivery, you may be sore for a few weeks. Your provider probably gave you some tips to help care for your bottom at home. Using a peri bottle with warm water to rinse after using the bathroom and using witch hazel pads are ways to help your bottom feel better.

Limiting physical activity: While you may want to return to your pre-pregnancy size, don't rush to exercise or get back in shape. Your healthcare provider will let you know when it's safe to exercise. Most people can begin walking or doing gentle movements a few days after giving birth. People who had a C-section birth may need to wait longer. Once you're able to exercise, begin slowly so you don't accidentally injure yourself.

Mental health support: Don't be afraid to ask for help and be patient with your emotions. The postpartum period can be challenging in so many ways. If you feel sad, overwhelmed, anxious or stressed, talk to a friend, your partner or your healthcare provider about it. There are many resources available to support you.

Some postpartum symptoms could be signs of a problem. You shouldn't ignore your symptoms or feel shame discussing how your recovery is going. If you have concerns either about how you're healing or how you feel, it's best to contact your healthcare provider. Some symptoms you should watch for include:

Heavy vaginal bleeding. This generally means you're filling a pad every hour for several hours. It can also mean that you're bleeding more each day instead of bleeding less.

Passing several large clots. A large clot is typically anything larger than a quarter. Passing one large clot is OK, but passing many could be a sign of a problem.

Fever higher than 101 degrees Fahrenheit (38 degrees Celsius).

New pains or an increase in pain. You should generally feel better over time, not worse.

Foul-smelling vaginal discharge.

Pain in your legs or ankles, especially with swelling.

Leaking pus or bloody discharge from your C-section incision.

Dizziness or changes to your vision.

Severe and persistent headaches.

Chest pains or shortness of breath.

The postpartum period is a time of adjustment and transition. People don't talk very much about the postpartum period, and it might leave you feeling lonely or unprepared. It's important to remember that you're not alone! While pregnancy seems to get

more attention, the postpartum period is just as important. You're learning how to deal with lots of physical and emotional changes, as well as trying to adjust to life with a newborn.

Some symptoms in postpartum are expected and nothing to worry about, while others can be signs that something else is going on. Be kind to yourself while you adjust, prioritize your well-being as much as you can and reach out for support from your healthcare provider if necessary. Even if you feel OK, it's important to attend all your postpartum checkups. This is where you can ask questions and where your provider can spot potential problems.

PART 2

PARENTING EARLY-CHILDHOOD

Emotional Development During Childhood

Helping Kids Develop Emotions at Every Age

Emotions are a big part of life, and they start developing in childhood. While kids feel emotions like adults, they often don't know how to show or handle them. If not guided properly, children may face issues like fear or sadness as they grow. This is why it's important to support their emotional and social growth early on.

Babies (Birth to 1 Year)

Babies show emotions like happiness, fear, and anger. They smile at comforting things like a gentle voice or a soft touch. Some babies learn to calm themselves by sucking their thumbs. When cared for with love, babies develop trust and feel safe.

How Parents Can Help:

Hold and cuddle your baby often.

Talk, sing, and read to them daily.

Respond to their needs with a calm and loving voice.

Spend lots of time with them to build a strong bond.

Toddlers (1-2 Years)

Toddlers start to notice how others feel. For example, they might get upset if another child cries. They also begin playing pretend, like pretending to cook. They feel big emotions but don't know how to explain them yet, so they need your help.

How Parents Can Help:

Encourage them to explore and be curious.

Teach them words for their feelings, like "happy" or "angry."

Show them how to share and take turns with others.

Stay calm when they have tantrums and comfort them afterward.

Preschoolers (3-5 Years)

Preschoolers learn to control their emotions better. They start sharing and playing with others, and they use their imagination a lot. They also begin understanding teamwork and taking turns.

How Parents Can Help:

Help them trust other adults, like teachers or family members.

Let them play with other kids and encourage teamwork.

Praise them when they manage their feelings well.

Play games or do activities that teach about feelings.

School-Age Kids (6-12 Years)

As kids grow, they feel more complex emotions and start learning how to handle them. They can tell what's an appropriate way to show feelings but may still need guidance. Learning to manage emotions is very important at this stage.

How Parents Can Help:

Teach them to recognize and name their feelings.

Help them figure out what causes their emotions and how to handle them.

Show them how to react calmly to tough situations.

Make them feel safe to talk about their feelings.

When kids feel safe and supported, they learn to manage their emotions better. By showing them love and teaching them how to handle feelings, you're helping them grow into emotionally healthy adults.

How can you Develop Social and Emotional Skills in your Kids?

While genetics influence how a child's brain is wired from birth, experiences and learning shape how the brain grows and develops.

One key factor in emotional development is observation. Children learn by watching. If they see you sharing, showing gratitude, and expressing feelings positively, they will learn to do the same when interacting with others.

The Power of Observation

Children imitate what they see. To set a good example:

Use polite words like "please" and "thank you."

Praise your child when they show good behaviour, like helping or sharing.

Create a positive environment where your child feels safe to express their emotions.

By modelling kindness and understanding, you teach your child empathy and emotional competence. This helps them grow into generous and thoughtful individuals.

Reinforcement and Emotional Intelligence

Rewarding positive behaviour helps children feel good about themselves and encourages them to repeat those actions. For example, giving a treat after cleaning up teaches them that this behaviour is valued.

To boost empathy and emotional intelligence:

Ask your child how they feel, like, "How did you feel when you lost your toy?"

Encourage them to think about others' emotions by asking, "How do you think Naina felt when you took her toy?"

This helps children understand the impact of their actions on others and develop emotional awareness.

The Importance of Play and Cooperation

Playing with other children helps kids learn cooperation and social skills. While toddlers may find it hard to share or wait their turn, these abilities improve with age and practice. As they interact, children also develop problem-solving skills, learning to negotiate and compromise.

Even conflicts during play are valuable, as they teach children how to manage disagreements and work with others.

The Role of Rewards and Punishments

Rewarding good behaviour makes it more likely to happen again. For example, if a child is praised for cleaning their room, they are more likely to do it in the future. On the other hand, punishment reduces the chance of unwanted behaviour.

What Kids Observe Matters

Children learn not only from their parents but also from siblings, peers, and even media like TV, mobile games, and the internet. This is why it's crucial to ensure they are exposed to positive behaviors.

Parents can model responsible actions by:

Showing patience and understanding.

Demonstrating respectful and kind behaviour.

Responding to situations in appropriate ways.

When kids grow up in a nurturing environment, they are more likely to feel confident, secure, and capable of handling challenges in life.

Early Attachment or Childhood Attachment:

What is attachment? Why it is important?

Attachment is a fundamental emotion that forms the foundation of every healthy relationship. It represents a deep and lasting emotional bond between two individuals, where both seek closeness and feel secure. In childhood, healthy attachment ensures that a child trusts their caregiver to meet their needs for food, comfort, stimulation, and care. This sense of security allows the child to explore their environment, develop confidence, and build positive self-esteem. Adults who experienced secure attachments as children are more likely to form fulfilling relationships later in life.

Conversely, poor attachment can result in anxiety, insecurity, and low self-esteem. Children who cannot rely on their caregivers to respond to their needs often struggle to form trust and confidence. Early attachment experiences are critical, as they lay the groundwork for later social and emotional development and mental health. These early bonds often influence an individual's behavior and relationships well into adulthood, serving as a model for how they interact with others. Secure attachment enables both children and adults to manage emotions, maintain relationships, and handle stress effectively, while also fostering trust, autonomy, and self-esteem. Although insecure attachment does not necessarily lead to disorders, it can create challenges such as difficulty trusting others, managing emotions, or maintaining self-confidence.

Attachment develops in stages. Studies show that by seven to nine months, babies typically form a specific attachment to one primary caregiver, and by ten months, they develop multiple attachments. These bonds begin to form when caregivers respond appropriately to an infant's needs, such as smiling in response to the baby's smile or cuddling when the baby cries. Interestingly, the strength of attachment is not determined by the amount of time spent with the baby but by the caregiver's ability to respond accurately to the baby's cues. This responsiveness helps establish a child's sense of security and acts as a blueprint for future social relationships.

Children who feel attached to a caregiver seek closeness and comfort during times of distress, illness, or fatigue. A strong attachment helps them regulate negative emotions during stressful situations and explore their environment confidently, even in the presence of challenges. Attachment is a critical developmental milestone that continues to play an essential role throughout life. In adulthood, attachment influences how individuals manage the complexities of intimate relationships, especially parent-child bonds, and how they perceive themselves.

Parents significantly influence their child's attachment patterns, which, in turn, impact the child's physical, emotional, and psychological well-being. For example, during illness, a child's behavior and the parent's response are often shaped by their respective attachment styles. Poor attachment can manifest in various challenges, such as behavioral difficulties, feeding problems, infant crying, poor eye contact, and developmental delays. Conditions like autism and ADHD are also linked to attachment patterns, making it a vital consideration in paediatric care. Attachment is equally important in addressing child protection and substitute care.

The consequences of inadequate childhood attachment are far-reaching. It not only affects the individual but also poses a significant burden on society. Poor attachment in childhood is associated with adult physical and psychological ill-health, contributing to major causes of mortality. It is a key factor in intergenerational parenting difficulties and increases the risk of substance abuse, temper problems, homelessness, early pregnancy, and criminal behavior. The issue is not whether children form attachments but whether their relationships provide a sense of safety, reliability, and value.

Addressing attachment issues is critical, as the legacy of inadequate childhood attachment affects individuals, families, and public services. A nurturing and responsive caregiving environment can positively shape a child's emotional development, setting them on a path toward healthier relationships and greater resilience in the face of life's challenges.

Some Studies and Researches Done on this

Research by Harry Harlow, John Bowlby, and Mary Ainsworth has significantly contributed to our understanding of attachment and its impact on child development. In the 1950s, Harlow conducted a series of groundbreaking experiments with monkeys. He separated newborn monkeys from their mothers and presented them with two surrogate mothers: one made of wire mesh that dispensed milk, and the other made of soft cloth but without milk. The baby monkeys overwhelmingly preferred the soft, cuddly cloth mother, even though she didn't provide nourishment. They spent most of their time clinging to her and only went to the wire mother when they needed to feed. This experiment challenged the prevailing belief that babies form attachments only to those who provide nourishment, highlighting the importance of comfort and security in maternal-infant bonding for healthy psychological development.

John Bowlby, building on Harlow's work, developed attachment theory. He defined attachment as the affectionate bond or tie that a child forms with their primary caregiver, typically the mother. Bowlby argued that this bond is essential for a child's normal social and emotional development. He introduced the concept of a "secure base," which refers to the caregiver providing a sense of safety and security, allowing the child to explore their environment with confidence. Bowlby emphasized two key elements for a healthy attachment: the caregiver must be responsive to the child's physical, social, and emotional needs, and there must be mutually enjoyable interactions between the caregiver and the child.

Mary Ainsworth, in her research, sought to understand whether children differ in the ways they form attachments, and if so, how. She developed the "Strange Situation" procedure to study parent-child attachment. In this experiment, a mother and her infant were placed in a room with toys, where the infant had the opportunity to explore. After a while, a stranger entered the room, and the mother left the baby with the stranger. After a brief separation, the mother returned to comfort the child. Ainsworth observed the children's reactions to the separation and reunion, identifying four attachment types: secure, avoidant, resistant, and disorganized.

Secure attachment, the most common and healthiest type, occurs when the child prefers their parent over a stranger and uses the parent as a secure base for exploring their environment. These children were distressed when their caregiver left the room but were happy to be reunited when the caregiver returned. Securely attached children tend to have caregivers who are sensitive and responsive to their needs.

In contrast, avoidant attachment occurs when the child is indifferent to the parent's presence and does not use the parent as a secure base. These children show little distress when the parent leaves and are slow to react positively when the parent returns. Ainsworth suggested that children with avoidant attachment likely have caregivers who are insensitive to their needs.

Resistant attachment is characterized by clinginess and difficulty in exploring the environment. These children tend to become extremely distressed and angry when the parent leaves and are hard to comfort upon the parent's return. Resistant attachment is often the result of inconsistent caregiving, where the caregiver's responses to the child's needs are unpredictable.

Lastly, disorganized attachment is observed in children who exhibit erratic and confusing behavior. These children may run around in an unpredictable manner or even attempt to run away when the caregiver returns. Disorganized attachment is most commonly seen in children who have experienced abuse or severe neglect. Research has shown that abuse disrupts a child's ability to regulate emotions, which can lead to this disorganized attachment style

Attachment Disorders

Attachment disorders are conditions that can arise in young children who struggle to establish a deep emotional connection with their parent or primary caregiver. These issues occur when a child cannot form a meaningful bond with a caregiver, leading them to feel abandoned, isolated, powerless, or uncared for. Such feelings can cause the child to view the world as a dangerous and frightening place, and they may not trust others to meet their emotional needs.

Children with attachment issues fall on a spectrum, ranging from mild difficulties to more severe attachment disorders, such as Reactive Attachment Disorder (RAD) and Disinhibited Social Engagement Disorder (DSED), both of which are recognized in the Diagnostic and Statistical Manual of Mental Disorders (DSM). These disorders are common in children who have experienced trauma, abuse, frequent moves in foster care, or separation from their primary caregiver. These children may struggle with forming relationships and are often developmentally delayed. However, with the right tools, patience, and love, it is possible to repair attachment issues and help children form healthy, loving relationships.

Parenting a child with attachment issues can be emotionally exhausting and frustrating. It may feel like your efforts are not working, but with time, patience, and consistent effort, attachment disorders can be healed. It is important to stay calm and firm in your interactions with your child, teaching them that they are safe and can trust you. To support a child with attachment issues, it is essential to:

Have realistic expectations, recognizing that the process may take time and small steps of progress should be celebrated.

Stay patient, understanding that improvement may be slow, but focusing on small victories can create a safe environment for the child.

Foster a sense of humour, as joy and laughter can energize you and help repair attachment issues.

Take care of yourself by managing stress, getting rest, and finding time for personal breaks to recharge.

Find support from friends, family, and community resources.

Stay positive and hopeful, as children pick up on their caregivers' feelings, and a positive outlook can be encouraging to them.

For adoptive parents, attachment disorders can be particularly challenging, as the child may not be able to bond with them immediately. This does not mean the child lacks love for the adoptive parents; rather, their past experiences have made it difficult for them to trust and recognize the parents as sources of comfort. With time and consistent efforts, adoptive parents can build a strong bond with their child.

To make a child with attachment issues feel secure, it is crucial to establish a sense of safety and stability. Children with attachment issues feel unsafe in the world and keep their guard up to protect themselves, which prevents them from accepting love and support. To address this, caregivers should:

Set clear expectations and rules of behavior, responding consistently so the child knows what to expect and can rely on their caregivers.

Set limits and boundaries, which make the world feel more stable and predictable.

Stay calm when the child is upset or misbehaving, showing that their feelings are manageable.

Be available to reconnect after conflicts, reinforcing the child's trust that the caregiver will always be there.

Own up to mistakes and initiate repair when necessary, teaching the child that love is unconditional, even when mistakes are made.

Maintain predictable routines and schedules to provide comfort during transitions.

To help the child feel loved, caregivers can show love through consistent actions, such as rocking, cuddling, or holding, while respecting the child's comfort level. If the child has experienced trauma, it is important to proceed slowly, as they may be resistant to physical touch. Caregivers should also respond to the child's emotional age, as children with attachment issues often act younger than their age. It is helpful to use non-verbal methods of soothing and comforting.

Additionally, caregivers should help the child identify and express their emotions, reinforcing that all feelings are valid and teaching them healthy ways to express themselves. Spending quality, focused time with the child through play, conversation, and attention is vital in building a secure bond.

If the child's attachment issues are severe, seeking professional help is recommended. Consulting a paediatrician, child development specialist, or an organization that specializes in attachment disorders can provide the necessary guidance and support.

Childhood Pampering

Today, every parent strives to provide the best for their children, whether it's in terms of education, food, or basic needs. Often, parents want to spare their children from the hardships they themselves experienced, ensuring their children lack nothing. In this process, however, parents sometimes cross the line between caring for and over-pampering their children. This overindulgence can lead to a decay in moral values, as young people today often lack the basic ethics of life.

Pampering can take many forms, such as buying gifts, providing luxury, and fulfilling children's wants and needs. Out of love and affection, parents may intentionally or unintentionally spoil their children. To a certain extent, this doesn't harm the child, but when it goes too far, it reinforces negative behaviors. Many parents, for instance, buy toys when their child cries, which only teaches the child to cry every time they want something. This creates a belief that people around them should cater to their desires. Pampering also includes doing tasks for children that they are fully capable of doing themselves. In some households, especially in Indian families, parents or grandparents feed, bathe, make the beds, and even dress their children, even after the children are old enough to do these tasks independently. This leads to a dependent nature, preventing children from developing essential life skills like dressing, eating, or bathing on their own. It's important for parents to let children do these tasks, even if they make mistakes. Learning to perform these basic activities is just as important as potty training.

Another common habit, particularly in Indian households, is parents doing their children's homework for them when they ask for help. This extended parenting care, where parents continue to provide for children even when they no longer need it, can lead to physical and emotional delays. Research has shown that over-pampered children often seek attention from everyone around them. Parents should avoid over-pampering, but instead create an environment of love and learning while disciplining. Children must be taught essential moral values as they grow, ensuring they don't become a burden on society. When pampered too much, children may make unnecessary demands on society and try to live beyond their means, which creates social problems. On the other hand, well-trained children grow up to be responsible and productive citizens.

Love and affection are key to a child's development, as they play an essential role in discipline. When properly administered, love and discipline go hand in hand. Children need undivided attention, quality time, kind words, hugs, and reassurance from significant adults in their lives. They learn what love is from their parents and guardians, and they, in turn, learn to express love to others. Children who don't receive enough love at home are more likely to struggle with low self-esteem, depression, and hostility.

A balance of reward and punishment is crucial for effective discipline. It's easy to lose focus on rewarding good behavior when we're constantly trying to correct bad behavior. Love and discipline cannot be separated when raising a child. Here are some ways to pamper a child in the right manner:

Don't shower them with false praise: This doesn't mean scolding or raising your voice all the time, but calmly addressing what went wrong and how it can be resolved. Constant false praise will not motivate a child to push their limits.

Have one-on-one time: Spend quality time with your child, even if it's just 15 minutes a day. This helps build a good relationship and makes your child feel comfortable talking to you.

Bribe them with experiences, not material things: Instead of buying them gifts, engage in activities that you both enjoy. Fun activities will increase bonding and provide lasting memories.

Let them choose: Allow your child to make decisions instead of imposing what you think is best. This helps them feel motivated and develop a sense of responsibility.

Don't help when they can handle things on their own: If your child is capable of completing a task with a little push, don't unnecessarily step in. Let them try and succeed on their own.

Don't give in to every demand: Sometimes, children will ask for more than what you've agreed to. It's important to stick to the limits you've set and avoid giving in to their demands.

Listen intently: Always listen to your child, even if their thoughts seem trivial. Don't react negatively; instead, explain the reasons behind your actions.

Choose experiences as rewards: Encourage your child by rewarding them with experiences rather than material possessions. This teaches them the value of memories and experiences over things.

By striking a balance between love, discipline, and pampering, parents can ensure that their children grow up with a healthy sense of responsibility and self-worth.

Bonding with your Child

Bonding is a deep emotional attachment that forms between parents and their child. It drives parents to shower their baby with love and affection, to protect and care for them. Bonding is what motivates parents to wake up in the middle of the night to feed their hungry baby and respond attentively to their baby's various cries. Scientists continue to explore the complexities of bonding, but they know that these strong connections between parents and their children provide the first model for intimate relationships, foster a sense of security, and promote positive self-esteem. Additionally, a parent's responsiveness to an infant's signals plays a crucial role in the child's social and cognitive development.

Bonding is not an immediate process. It doesn't happen in a matter of minutes or within a fixed timeframe after birth. For many parents, bonding happens naturally through everyday caregiving. You may not even realize it's happening until you see your baby's first smile, and in that moment, you may feel overwhelmed with love and joy.

The process of bonding starts during pregnancy. As discussed in the context of parenthood during pregnancy, it often takes time to understand your child, and touch becomes an early form of communication. Babies respond to skin-to-skin contact, which is soothing for both the parent and the baby, promoting healthy growth and development. Eye contact also facilitates meaningful communication. Babies are drawn to human voices and begin vocalizing as they start their first efforts at communication.

They enjoy hearing descriptions of their activities and the world around them.

Bonding with your baby is one of the most rewarding parts of infant care. You can begin by cradling your baby, gently rocking, or stroking them. If both parents hold and touch the baby frequently, the baby will start to distinguish between their touch and that of others. Parents can also engage in skin-to-skin contact with the newborn during feeding or cradling, which enhances the bonding process.

Breastfeeding and bottle-feeding are natural opportunities for bonding. Infants respond to the smell, touch, and responsiveness of their parents. For adoptive parents, while bonding might take a bit longer, it is just as possible as with biological parents. Adopted babies can bond with their parents through love, care, and consistency.

Here are some early bonding activities to help nurture this connection:

Eating together

Giving them a bath

Talking about your day

Playing together

Being respectful and the same

Letting the child help

Cuddling

Showing love daily

Reading a story together

Baking and cooking

Going to the park

Colouring and painting

Gardening

Indoor picnics

Hosting a party for two

Visiting an orphanage and playing with other kids

Playing dress-up

Arts and crafts

Having a jam session with toy musical instruments

Going on a trek in the garden to find interesting items

Spending time with pets

Trying out interesting puzzles

Solving riddles

Watching clean family documentary movies

Reading moral stories

Sharing your culture, traditions, and ancestral history

Reading a story before bed

During dinner, sharing the best, worst, and weirdest parts of your day

Sharing stories from your childhood

Giving a compliment every day

Putting down your phone and making eye contact when speaking

Scheduling a weekly or monthly family game night

Making up nicknames for each other

Establishing a no-technology hour for the family

Looking through family photos

Doing a science experiment together

Learning something new together

Performing skits or dramas based on moral stories during special events or festivals

These bonding activities help foster a deeper connection between parents and children, creating lasting memories and reinforcing a secure emotional attachment.

Childhood Trauma

Trauma refers to a frightening, dangerous, or violent event that can have lasting emotional and physical effects on a person. These experiences can trigger strong emotions and physiological reactions that persist long after the event. Individuals may feel terror, helplessness, and experience physical symptoms such as a pounding heart, vomiting, or loss of bowel or bladder control. Children who experience traumatic stress are those who have been exposed to one or more traumatic events and develop reactions that continue to affect their daily lives long after the events have ended.

Traumatic reactions can include a range of responses such as intense emotional distress, depressive symptoms, anxiety, behavioral changes, difficulties with self-regulation, problems forming relationships or attachments, regression of previously acquired skills, attention and academic difficulties, nightmares, and sleep or eating disturbances. Physical symptoms like aches and pains can also occur. Children suffering from traumatic stress often exhibit these symptoms when reminded of the traumatic event. While stress reactions are common, when a child experiences traumatic stress, these reactions interfere with their ability to function and interact with others. No child is immune to the effects of trauma, and even infants and toddlers can experience traumatic stress. The way trauma manifests will vary based on the child's age and developmental stage.

If untreated, repeated exposure to trauma can affect the brain and nervous system, increasing health risks. Research shows that children who experience trauma are more likely to develop long-term health issues and may have a shorter life expectancy. Traumatic experiences often leave lasting reminders that can persist for years.

These reminders can be linked to aspects of the trauma, such as people, places, things, or situations associated with the event.

Fortunately, not all children who experience a traumatic event develop traumatic stress. Several factors contribute to a child's symptoms, including the severity of the event, proximity to it, the caregiver's reaction, and prior history of trauma. Protective factors at the child, family, and community levels can reduce the adverse effects of trauma. These factors include the child's environment, family support, and community resources. The culture, race, and ethnicity of the child and their family can also act as protective factors. Families and communities may have qualities or resources that help buffer the harmful effects of trauma.

Cultural influences often positively impact how children and families respond, recover, and heal from traumatic experiences. However, experiences of racism and discrimination can increase a child's risk of developing traumatic stress.

If a child is suffering from trauma, it's essential to seek professional help. Consulting a doctor and connecting with agencies specializing in trauma care can guide the healing process.

Importance of Nutrition and Physical activity during Early Childhood

Nutrition plays a crucial role in a child's development, particularly during the early years. Research has shown that early childhood nutrition is linked to both health and academic performance later in life. In fact, the importance of nutrition begins even before birth. Undernutrition during pregnancy can stunt fetal growth and lead to poor brain development, resulting in irreversible chronic illnesses.

Undernutrition in a breastfeeding mother can similarly negatively impact a child's development, especially in the first six months when breast milk is the sole source of nutrition. It's essential for soon-to-be and new mothers to consume a healthy, balanced diet full of vital nutrients for both their own health and the health of their child. The benefits of good nutrition are extensive, and several studies highlight key conclusions:

Breastfeeding and Nutrition: Mothers who follow a nutritious diet and breastfeed their children experience fewer and less severe cases of illnesses such as diarrhea, ear infections, and bacterial meningitis. This is because well-nourished children have enhanced immune systems, which help them fight infections more effectively.

Iron and Brain Development: Iron is a vital component of brain tissue, and iron deficiency can cause nerve impulses to move more slowly, potentially leading to permanent brain damage. In the first two years of life, iron deficiency is linked to behavior changes and delayed psychomotor development. However, too much iron can also cause problems.

Impact of Undernutrition: Undernutrition decreases a child's activity levels, social interactions, curiosity, and cognitive functioning. It may seem surprising, but what a child consumes in their early years can affect their learning abilities in the long term. Research has shown that breastfeeding leads to higher IQ, while iron deficiency correlates with reduced cognition and academic achievements later in life. Undernourished children are also more prone to illness, which can lead to missed school days and falling behind in their studies. School-age children who eat breakfast perform better on tests than those who skip it.

Following nutrition guidelines during pregnancy and early childhood is straightforward. However, as children begin to develop preferences for certain foods, it's important to respect their likes and dislikes while continuing to introduce new foods. Playful interactions like making silly faces or playing peek-a-boo can make mealtime more enjoyable, and in time, your toddler will start eating more independently.

Though it may take some time, your child will thank you later for fostering healthy eating habits early on.

Nutrition during Early Childhood

Achieving a healthy diet is about balancing the quality of the food consumed. There are five key factors that contribute to a healthy diet:

Adequacy: A diet must provide sufficient amounts of essential nutrients, including fiber and adequate calories, to support overall health.

Balance: A balanced diet occurs when you consume appropriate amounts of all nutrients without focusing too much on one while neglecting others.

Calorie Control: It is essential that the amount of energy you consume matches the energy you expend through daily activities to maintain healthy body weight.

Moderation: Moderation involves eating neither too much nor too little of any particular food, ensuring that no nutrient is over-consumed or under-consumed.

Variety: A varied diet includes different foods from each food group, ensuring that you receive a wide range of nutrients necessary for health.

A healthy diet prioritizes whole foods over processed options. Whole foods, which include fresh fruits, vegetables, grains, lean proteins, and healthy fats, provide essential nutrients such as vitamins, minerals, fiber, and proteins, all of which contribute to overall health. On the other hand, commercially prepared and fast foods often lack essential nutrients and are high in sugar, salt, and unhealthy fats, which are linked to the development of diseases such as heart disease, stroke, cancer, obesity, and diabetes.

An adequate diet favours nutrient-dense foods, which provide a high concentration of essential nutrients per calorie. These include fruits, vegetables, lean meats, fish, low-fat dairy, and whole grains. Nutrient-dense foods help with weight management while providing necessary nutrients.

Moderation is key for maintaining health. Regular consumption of nutrient-poor foods, such as fast food, can lead to health complications, but occasional indulgence in moderation, within the context of an otherwise healthy diet, should not have a significant impact. Monitoring portion sizes is also important for weight management, as excess energy from food can lead to weight gain over time.

Variety ensures that you consume adequate amounts of all essential nutrients by eating foods from all the food groups. A varied diet prevents nutrient imbalances and encourages trying new foods, which can be both enjoyable and beneficial.

When developing a healthy diet, it is important to integrate all these principles. Introducing variety into your diet can still result in overconsumption of high-calorie, nutrient-poor foods if not balanced with moderation and calorie control. Using all of these principles together will help achieve lasting health benefits.

Meal pattern for Infants

Breastfeeding is recommended for the first six months of a baby's life, as breast milk or formula provides all the necessary nutrition. However, between 4 to 6 months, most babies are ready to begin solid foods in addition to breast milk or formula.

Signs that your baby is ready for solids include:

Holding their head up.

Sitting with little support.

Bringing their hands or toys to their mouth.

Leaning toward food and opening their mouth wide to indicate hunger.

Leaning back or turning away to signal fullness.

When introducing solid foods, start with single-ingredient options without added sugar or salt. Wait 3 to 5 days between introducing new foods to observe any reactions like diarrhea, rash, or vomiting. Begin with pureed or mashed foods, which are easier for babies to swallow, and gradually introduce thicker and lumpier textures as they develop oral skills.

Be mindful of choking hazards. Prepare foods in a way that makes them easy to dissolve in the mouth and avoid foods that require chewing. Feed small portions and always supervise your baby while eating. Here are some tips for preparing solid foods:

Mix cereals or mashed grains with breast milk, formula, or water for smooth textures.

Mash or puree vegetables, fruits, and other foods until smooth.

Cook hard fruits and vegetables, like apples and carrots, until soft enough to mash.

Remove bones, skin, and fat from meats and fish before cooking.

Cut fruits and vegetables into small pieces or thin slices, removing seeds or pits.

Cut cylindrical foods like hot dogs or cheese into small strips, and small spherical foods like grapes or berries into pieces.

Between 8 to 10 months, most babies can handle small amounts of finely chopped, soft finger foods like soft fruits, vegetables, pasta, cheese, and well-cooked meats. At this stage, you can also start offering water with meals, encouraging a habit that will last a lifetime. Limit juice consumption to no more than 4 ounces per day, and avoid juice for babies under 1 year old.

It is important to wait until your baby has tried basic foods before introducing potential allergens, such as peanuts, eggs, dairy, shellfish, and soy. Research suggests that introducing allergenic foods early may reduce the risk of allergies. Always try these foods at home and have an antihistamine on hand in case of a reaction.

Avoid giving cow's milk or honey to babies before age 1. Cow's milk does not provide enough iron, and honey can cause infant botulism. Additionally, avoid choking hazards like hard foods, seeds, nuts, popcorn, and hard candy. For peanut butter, spread it thinly or mix it with other foods to make it smoother.

Feeding time should be enjoyable and relaxed. Talk to your baby during meals, and when your baby can sit without help, use a highchair with safety straps. Let your baby explore foods and encourage self-feeding with a spoon. Gradually transition your baby from bottle-feeding to drinking from a cup around 9 months.

Your baby's stools may change as they begin eating solids, becoming more solid and varied in colour and odor. This is normal, but if stools are excessively loose or contain mucus, consult your child's doctor.

While breast milk or formula provides all the hydration your baby needs, a small amount of water can be offered once solids are introduced, particularly in hot weather. Limit water to no more than 8 ounces per day. If your water is fluoridated, drinking it can also help prevent tooth decay.

Early mealtimes are a great opportunity to encourage good eating habits. Eating together as a family has positive effects on child development. Offer a variety of healthy foods, and pay attention to your baby's hunger cues. Don't overfeed, and if you have concerns about your baby's nutrition, consult with their doctor.

Meal pattern for Children

Vegetables and Fruits

At least one of the two required components of a snack should be a vegetable or fruit. Serve a variety of fruits, focusing on whole fruits rather than juices. Limit juice to one serving per day. Provide at least one serving each of dark green leafy vegetables, red and orange vegetables, beans and peas (legumes), starchy vegetables, and other vegetables each week.

Grains

Provide at least two servings of whole grains per day, with at least one being a whole grain.

Meat and Meat Alternatives

Serve only lean meats, nuts, and legumes. Limit servings of processed meats to no more than one serving per week.

Milk

Serve only unflavoured milk. Non-dairy milk substitutes that are nutritionally equivalent to milk may be served for children with medical or special dietary needs.

Sugar

Yogurt should contain no more than 2-3 grams of sugar per 6 ounces.

Breakfast cereals should contain no more than 6 grams of sugar per dry ounce.

Avoid serving foods with added sugars, such as sweet toppings like honey, jam, syrups, or mix-ins with yogurt, as well as sugar-sweetened beverages.

Miscellaneous

Limit deep-fried foods and purchased pre-fried foods to no more than one serving per week.

Avoid frozen foods as much as possible.

Incorporate seasonal and locally produced foods into meals.

Beverages

Only unflavoured, unsweetened, non-fat milk can be served to children 2 years of age or older.

No beverages with added sweeteners (natural or artificial) should be served, including sports drinks, sweet teas, juice drinks with added sugars, flavoured milk, soda, and diet drinks.

A maximum of one serving of 100% fruit juice is allowed per day.

Clean and safe drinking water must be readily available at all times, indoors and outdoors, and with meals and snacks.

Beating Unhealthy Foods

Added Sugars: Limit added sugars found in items like brown sugar, corn syrup, and honey. Opt for cereals with minimal added sugars and avoid sodas and other drinks with added sugars. If your child drinks juice, ensure it is 100% juice with no added sugars.

Saturated Fats: Saturated fats are primarily from animal sources like red meat, poultry, butter, and full-fat dairy. Replace these with vegetable and nut oils that provide essential fatty acids and vitamin E.

Salt: Processed foods such as pizza, pasta dishes, and soup often contain high levels of salt. Encourage snacking on fruits and vegetables instead of chips and cookies, and choose low-sodium products when available.

Avoid Packed and Preserved Foods: These can affect both physical and mental development, leading to issues such as obesity, diabetes, and reduced brain development.

Tips for Developing Healthy Eating Patterns

Mealtime Environment: Keep mealtimes pleasant and free from stress. Avoid turning food into a source of conflict. Do not force your child to eat, as this can lead to negative associations with food.

Meal Preparation: Avoid preparing different meals for each child or family member. Children tend to do better when they are hungry and a meal is ready.

Offer Limited Choices: Give your child one or two specific meal options rather than an open-ended question like, "What do you want for lunch?" This prevents indecisiveness and ensures balanced meals.

Involve Children in Cooking: Preparing meals together can be a fun and memorable experience, encouraging children to try new foods.

Avoid Bribing: Do not bribe children with dessert in exchange for eating vegetables. This teaches them that some foods are better than others and can lead to a dislike for healthy foods.

Quality of Food

Food quality is determined by its nutrient density—foods that provide significant amounts of essential nutrients relative to the calories they contain. High-quality foods, like fruits, vegetables, and whole grains, provide more nutritional value than empty-calorie foods like sugary sodas.

The Challenge of Choosing Foods

Several factors influence food choices, including:

Taste, Texture, and Appearance: Personal preferences can impact food choices, and some healthy foods may not be immediately appealing.

Economics: Limited access to fresh fruits and vegetables can lead to reliance on convenience foods.

Early Food Experiences: Childhood exposure to different foods can shape adult eating habits.

Habits: Routines can either promote or hinder optimal health, such as choosing fast food over home-cooked meals.

Culture: Cultural traditions and celebrations often involve specific foods, influencing food choices.

Geography: A person's location can limit or expand food choices based on availability.

Social Factors: Peer pressure can influence eating habits, especially in social settings.

Health Concerns: Dietary restrictions due to allergies or health issues affect food choices.

Emotions: Emotional stress can either lead to overeating or loss of appetite.

Green Food/Sustainability Choices: Growing awareness of environmental issues has led many people to choose sustainable, cruelty-free, or locally grown foods.

By understanding these factors, individuals can make healthier food choices that support both physical and emotional well-being.

Impact of Physical Activity during Early Childhood

Healthy active living, which encompasses eating nutritious foods, staying physically active, and getting enough rest, is essential for a child's growth and development. Early childhood is a critical period to instill these healthy habits. Research shows that the way children eat, move, and sleep influences their health both now and in the future. Starting these habits early helps prevent the establishment of unhealthy patterns later in life.

The Importance of Physical Activity in Early Childhood

Good physical activity habits should begin early in a child's life. Even infants can engage in physical activities that promote healthy growth. For instance, infants should spend time on the floor, allowing them to reach, kick, and eventually crawl, which are crucial developmental milestones. Activities that limit movement, like excessive screen time or extended stroller use, can hinder development. Physical activity for young children means allowing them to move freely and play with others.

Physical activity has a wide range of benefits, including promoting healthy body composition, strong bones, and improved cardiovascular fitness. It also enhances motor skills, concentration, and cognitive development. By engaging in physical activities, children not only develop physically but also emotionally and socially. For example, active play with caregivers can improve communication skills, while playing with peers fosters friendship, teamwork, and conflict resolution.

Motor Skills Development

Motor skills are divided into locomotors (e.g., walking), stability (e.g., balance), and manipulative (e.g., throwing) skills. While free play is important, guided activities are necessary for children to develop advanced motor skills, such as those needed for team sports. Without mastering these skills, children may lose interest in physical activity, leading to barriers in later participation. It's important to focus on creating an environment that encourages mastery rather than just winning.

Cognitive and Language Development

Physical activity has been shown to positively influence cognitive development. Research suggests that increased physical activity can improve executive function, language skills, and spatial awareness. For example, children who engage in moderate to vigorous physical activity show improvements in literacy and phonological awareness, such as rhyming and alliteration. Physical activity can also promote self-regulation, which is beneficial for learning and behavior control.

The Role of Caregivers and Role Models

Children learn by observing adults, so caregivers must model healthy behaviors. If a caregiver demonstrates physical activity or tries new foods, children are more likely to adopt those behaviors themselves. For instance, children are more likely to try new foods if they see their parents eating those foods. Similarly, children who see their parents being physically active are more likely to engage in physical activity themselves.

Health Benefits of Physical Activity

Regular physical activity in early childhood helps prevent many health problems, such as obesity, high blood pressure, bad cholesterol, and bone health issues. Active children are less prone to chronic health conditions like heart disease, diabetes, and depression. They also tend to have stronger immune systems and better overall health.

Recommendations for Physical Activity by Age Group

Infants: Engage in at least 30 minutes of tummy time spread throughout the day while awake. Provide sensory activities to support development.

Toddlers: Aim for at least 180 minutes of physical activity at any intensity, including moderate to vigorous activities. Interactive play without many toys is ideal to stimulate both physical and mental growth.

School-aged Children: Spend at least 180 minutes in physical activity, with at least 60 minutes of moderate to vigorous activity. This can include activities like running, playing on the playground, or sports.

Types of Physical Activity

For Preschoolers:

Moderate-intensity activities: Games like tag, dancing, swimming, or playground activities.

Vigorous-intensity activities: Activities like running, skipping, or gymnastics.

Muscle-strengthening: Tug of war, climbing, gymnastics.

Bone-strengthening: Hopping, jumping, and skipping.

For School-aged Children:

Moderate-intensity activities: Brisk walking, swimming, or playing sports like basketball and softball.

Vigorous-intensity activities: Running, sports like soccer, or vigorous dancing.

Muscle-strengthening: Resistance exercises, yoga, climbing.

Bone-strengthening: Jumping rope, running, and sports that involve rapid jumping.

By promoting healthy eating habits and regular physical activity from an early age, caregivers can set children up for a lifetime of good health and well-being.

Parenting during Early Childhood

Things to Avoid during Parenting your Kids

Parenting is one of the most physically and emotionally demanding jobs in the world, as it involves more than just providing a roof over a child's head and food in his/her stomach. You're attempting to develop a child who is courageous, independent, kind, hardworking and a humane individual, but though there are many things we get right when it comes to parenting, there are also some that may do more harm than good. There is a fine line between wanting the best for your child and pushing them knowingly in the wrong direction. Frequently, parents are ignorant of mental harm they are inflicting on their children and it is common for them to declare that 'everything is for the best' when in reality they are actually harming their children's minds. Being a parent is tough no matter how conscientious and alert we are, mistakes are inevitable. However, both parents and children have a lot to learn in the process. You can avoid some common parenting mistakes if you know what to look for. By learning to overcome these common parenting mistakes, you will be one step closer to be becoming a more effective parent.

Minimizing your kid's feelings- It's important for children to understand that expressing and talking about their emotions is a healthy and natural part of life. When parents use phrases like "Don't be so upset about it" or "It's not that important," it can unintentionally convey the idea that emotions are insignificant or should be ignored. Instead, parents can validate their child's feelings and guide them toward managing their emotions effectively. For example, if a child feels frightened during a loud storm, a parent might say, "I can see that you're feeling scared right now." Then, they can gently ask, "What do you think might help you feel better?" This approach encourages children to identify and practice coping strategies. Over time, this helps them develop the ability to brainstorm and implement solutions, building their emotional resilience and problem-solving skills.

Not listening to the kids- Children often just want to feel heard and have the opportunity to express their emotions. Unfortunately, one of the most common mistakes parents make is overlooking this need. To foster a healthy relationship, it's essential for parents to take the time to truly listen to their children. Giving them your full attention shows them they are valued and respected. If something is bothering your child, take it seriously, even if it seems minor to you. When they come to you, focus on listening rather than immediately trying to fix the issue. Strong relationships are built on mutual respect, trust, cooperation, problem-solving, and shared responsibility. If you only listen with the intent to critique, teach, or solve the problem, your child may feel dismissed and start to withdraw emotionally. Instead, validate their feelings and give them the space to express themselves. By allowing them to process their emotions, you're helping them feel understood and supported, which can significantly improve their emotional well-being.

Ignoring your child's emotional needs- Neglecting a child's emotional needs is a form of abandonment that can lead to deep-seated personality challenges, often affecting their mental and emotional well-being in the long term. This type of neglect doesn't always involve physical absence; a child can feel unloved or overlooked even through subtle actions or a lack of response. When a child is upset, even over something seemingly small, it's crucial for parents to provide comfort, reassurance, and care. Whether it's offering a hug when they're unwell, celebrating their small achievements, standing up for them, or simply being present, these gestures reinforce their sense of security and belonging. Failing to meet these emotional needs may push children to seek support elsewhere, which might not always be beneficial or safe for them. As a parent, consistently showing love, empathy, and support helps build a strong emotional foundation that allows children to thrive.

Always saving them from failure- As parents, it's natural to want to shield our children from struggles and solve their problems for them. However, consider this: if your child is struggling in school, simply giving them the answers to their homework won't help in the long run. You won't be there to guide them during tests or real-world challenges, and they'll miss out on the opportunity to learn and grow independently. Failure is an essential part of success. It teaches resilience, problem-solving, and perseverance—skills that are crucial for navigating life's ups and downs. By allowing children to experience setbacks and supporting them as they learn from those experiences, parents can help them develop the strength and determination they need to overcome obstacles and achieve their goals.

Overindulging your kids- kids love getting new things, and parents enjoy making them happy. However, research shows that constantly giving children whatever they want can hinder the development of critical skills like self-discipline and mental resilience. You want your kids to grow up knowingly that it's possible to achieve what they want if they work for it. Parents can teach their kids learn self-control by setting clear rules for things like finishing homework before screen time or doing chores to boost allowance, so they can buy things on their own, while knowing they earned it. A mature adult is someone who respects other's choice as well and can respectfully take a 'no'. But if you don't teach your kid the value of someone else's or even your 'no', they can grow up to be entitled and selfish.

Not letting your child explore- From the moment they are born, children are constantly learning. They begin by observing your face, understanding your expressions, and slowly developing the ability to connect with you. As they grow into pre-teens, play becomes their primary way of learning and discovering the world around them. Naturally, this can sometimes lead to bumps, bruises, or small setbacks. However, these experiences shouldn't be a reason to overly guard or restrict them. Over protectiveness can stifle their curiosity and discourage them from trying new things or learning from their mistakes. Whether it's through sports, academics, or other activities, children need the freedom to explore and grow. By allowing them to take risks and navigate challenges, you help them build confidence, resilience, and a lifelong love of learning.

Making comparisons between your child and others- One of the most harmful mistakes parents can make is comparing their child to others, especially when it comes to academic performance or other achievements. When children start school, their grades are often compared to those of their classmates. However, constantly pointing out that others are doing better will not improve your child's performance; instead, it can damage their self-confidence and negatively impact their ability to succeed. Rather than comparing, parents should take the time to sit with their child, understand the challenges they are facing, and work together to find solutions. Comparing children to others can leave lasting scars on their personality, leading to issues like inferiority complexes, low self-esteem, a lack of self-love, and the belief that they will never be good enough. Parents often compare their children in various aspects, such as career choices, marital status, religious beliefs, or test scores. It's crucial to remember that every child is unique, with their own strengths and weaknesses. Instead of comparing, celebrate their individuality and provide the support they need to thrive. Recognizing and nurturing your child's distinct qualities can help them develop a healthy sense of self-worth and emotional well-being.

Expecting perfection -It's natural for parents to want their children to aim high and excel in everything they do. However, setting unrealistic expectations can do more harm than good, often leading to issues with self-esteem and confidence later in life. To help your child develop mental strength, ensure that your expectations are both realistic and supportive. Even if they don't meet those goals, the setbacks they encounter can teach them valuable lessons about perseverance, growth, and success. Pushing a child toward perfectionism can create a relentless cycle of striving for more, often leaving them with feelings of dissatisfaction and failure. Over time, this pressure can lead to mental health challenges like stress, anxiety, and sadness. It's important for parents to recognize that it's okay for their child not to be flawless. They don't always need to earn the highest grades, win every award, or excel in every activity. By embracing their imperfections and celebrating their efforts rather than just the outcomes, you can help your child develop a healthier mindset. Acknowledging that success doesn't require perfection allows them to focus on growth, resilience, and self-acceptance, laying the foundation for a balanced and fulfilling life.

Over protectiveness- Over protectiveness may ease your anxiety as a parent, but it can hinder your child's growth and development. Shielding them from challenges and obstacles might seem like a way to keep them safe, but it prevents them from learning essential life skills. Instead of acting as a constant guardian, think of yourself as a guide—someone who supports and advises but allows them to navigate their own path. By letting your children face life's ups and downs, you give them the chance to build confidence in their ability to overcome challenges. While it may be difficult to let go, these experiences are crucial for fostering resilience, independence, and self-reliance. Providing your child with the space to explore and make mistakes is one of the greatest gifts you can offer, preparing them to handle whatever life may bring.

Making sure they always feel comfortable- Children often face moments of discomfort, especially when they are asked to try something new—whether it's tasting new foods, making new friends, starting a new sport, or even moving to a new home and school. These situations can feel daunting, but just like experiencing failure, embracing discomfort is an important step in building mental strength. Encourage your children to step outside their comfort zone and try new things. The beginning is often the hardest part, so help them get started by offering support and guidance. Once they take that first step, they may discover that the challenge isn't as overwhelming as they thought. In fact, they might even find that they're good at it and enjoy the experience. By allowing your children to face discomfort, you're helping them develop resilience and confidence in their ability to handle life's challenges.

Not empathizing with your kids- When your child faces a challenging situation, one of the most impactful things you can do is to empathize before reacting. Take a moment to put yourself in their shoes. If they're crying, upset, frustrated, or angry, remember that they are not trying to make things harder for you. Instead, they are struggling with emotions they may not yet know how to manage. In these moments, it's important to respond with patience and understanding. Gently invite them to sit beside you, offer a comforting gesture like rubbing their back, and say something reassuring like, "It's okay, take your time." By showing empathy, you help your child feel supported and give them the space they need to process their emotions. This compassionate approach teaches them that it's okay to experience difficult feelings and that they are not alone in navigating them.

Trying too hard to raise a perfect child- One of the most common mistakes that first-time parents often make is trying to raise a "perfect" child by imposing too many restrictions and strict rules. While it's natural to want the best for your child, constantly pushing them to behave in a specific way and rigidly controlling their actions can create distance between you and them. Instead, focus on setting clear guidelines that provide structure, but make sure they are flexible enough to adapt to your child's unique needs and responses. The goal is not to control your child, but to discipline them in a way that encourages understanding, growth, and cooperation. By maintaining a balance of consistency and flexibility, you foster a healthier relationship and help your child develop the ability to make good decisions independently.

Using guilt to manipulate a child into doing something—often through emotional blackmail—is a tactic some parents may resort to. However, this can be deeply damaging to a child's confidence and self-esteem. Over time, guilt can make them question themselves and feel inadequate. A healthier approach is for parents to have open, honest conversations with their children. Instead of blaming or shaming, explain your expectations clearly and respectfully. This helps the child understand the reasons behind your requests and encourages them to take responsibility without feeling burdened by guilt. By fostering a positive, supportive dialogue, you can guide your child in a way that strengthens their self-worth and improves their ability to meet expectations.

Not setting parent-child boundaries- It's important for children to learn how to make their own decisions, but they also need to understand that as a parent, you are the one setting boundaries. For instance, if you set a curfew for your 12-year-old, it's essential to enforce it consistently. Kids who grow up to be mentally strong tend to have parents who recognize the importance of clear boundaries and follow through with them. When rules are frequently negotiated or relaxed, it can create power struggles between you and your child. Instead, maintaining consistency and being firm with your expectations teaches children responsibility and respect for limits, helping them develop the self-discipline they need to thrive. By balancing independence with structure, you can guide them in making good decisions while reinforcing the importance of accountability.

Assuming that children will always agree on everything- Some children are raised by parents who do not allow them to express differing thoughts or opinions. These parents may label their children as stubborn, rebellious, ignorant, or worse, simply for questioning or offering an alternative perspective. Often, such parents do not tolerate any form of questioning, as they view it as a challenge to their authority or beliefs. In extreme cases, toxic religious parents may even call their children "possessed," while other dysfunctional parents might use equally harmful labels like "crazy." This kind of parenting is harmful because it stifles the child's ability to think independently and develop their own identity. When children are made to feel inferior or wrong for having their own thoughts, they are less likely to express themselves openly in the future. This creates an environment of tension and fear, making it difficult for the child to develop healthy communication skills or a positive sense of self. Instead of fostering understanding, this approach undermines the child's confidence and emotional well-being.

Aspiring to live out your unfulfilled dreams- Just because your child has more opportunities and better resources than you did doesn't mean you should push them to achieve what you couldn't. Every child is unique, with their own preferences, talents, and passions. Trying to shape your child's interests to match your own desires can limit their ability to explore and pursue what truly excites them. Forcing them to follow your path, rather than encouraging them to find their own, can have a significant negative impact on their mental health. It can lead to feelings of resentment, anxiety, and a lack of self-identity. Instead, support your child in discovering their own passions and interests, allowing them the freedom to develop their unique talents and live a fulfilling life on their terms.

Telling your kid that they are always right- Pampering children is a natural instinct for many parents, but overdoing it can have negative consequences. If children are constantly told they are always right, it can lead to overconfidence and a lack of self-awareness. It's important for children to understand that their actions have consequences and that they can make mistakes, just like anyone else. Hiding or covering up a child's mistakes only encourages them to repeat them in the future. Instead, it's more beneficial to guide them in recognizing where they went wrong and help them take responsibility for their actions. Teaching children to own up to their mistakes fosters accountability, humility, and growth. By doing so, you help them develop a stronger sense of self and a healthier approach to handling challenges in the future.

"Complete this homework, or else you will have to cry later !"

Teaching children discipline is essential, but it doesn't have to come through punishment or causing them distress. Many parents confuse authority with punishment, often focusing more on reprimanding misbehavior rather than helping children develop the skills needed for self-control. Discipline should not be about forcing children to do what we want. Instead, the focus should be on teaching them how to pause, reflect, and make thoughtful choices. By guiding them to understand the consequences of their actions and helping them learn how to make better decisions, you equip them with the tools to manage their behavior in a positive and constructive way. This approach fosters independence, responsibility, and emotional maturity, rather than fear or resentment.

Fighting with your partner in front of your kid- The foundation of a child's understanding of healthy relationships is built at home. If there is constant conflict between parents or caregivers, it can significantly impact a child's mental health. Children are highly impressionable, and witnessing frequent arguments or aggression can lead them to adopt similar behaviors as they grow older. It's important to model respectful communication, problem-solving, and emotional regulation in front of your child. When they see healthy conflict resolution and cooperation between parents, they are more likely to internalize these behaviors and carry them into their own relationships in the future. Creating a peaceful and supportive environment at home helps children develop a secure foundation for emotional well-being and positive social interactions.

Preaching without practising- It's easy to give long lectures about morals and values, but the real impact comes from practicing what we preach. Children see us as their role models and often imitate our behavior. If you tell your child that eating junk food all the time is unhealthy or that excessive screen time is bad, make sure you are modelling those behaviors as well. If you want your child to make healthier food choices, start by making those choices yourself.

Instead of just telling them what to eat, involve them in the process and teach them why certain foods are better than others. Explaining the benefits of healthy eating, rather than simply labelling foods as "good" or "bad," helps children understand the reasoning behind their choices. This empowers them to make wise decisions on their own and fosters a positive attitude toward healthy living.

Forcing to comply with socially established rules and standards- Children often express themselves in unique ways, and some may be considered "different" according to societal norms. However, being "different" does not mean being "wrong." Society often imposes rules about what is acceptable, but these norms should not restrict your child's ability to explore their interests and express themselves freely. For example, if a boy enjoys cooking—a hobby often stereotyped as more suited for girls—he may face criticism or exclusion. As a parent, it's important to support your child in pursuing their passions, regardless of whether they align with traditional gender roles or expectations. Rather than forcing your child to conform to societal standards, help them embrace and enhance their individuality. Encouraging them to explore their interests helps them build confidence and self-acceptance, fostering a healthy sense of identity that isn't constrained by external expectations.

Not helping them in understanding the outside world- As your child grows, their exposure to the world outside your family and home increases. It's essential to guide them with a sense of direction and understanding about how to interact with and perceive the world. This helps them develop into smarter, more open-minded individuals. Engage in conversations about what your child may be seeing on the news, hearing from peers, or reading on social media. Whether it's something positive or negative, it's important to address their questions and clear up any confusion. It's far better to teach them about both the right and wrong aspects of the outside world yourself than to let someone else, or the world at large, provide misinformation. If your child has doubts and you don't answer them, they may seek answers elsewhere, which may not always be accurate or healthy. This could mislead them, and later, you may end up blaming society for influencing your child negatively. While some parents may overreact and shield their children from society, this can be equally harmful. Eventually, they will face the world on their own, and by then, it may be too late for you to guide them. Therefore, it's crucial to provide the right teaching at the right age and time, ensuring your child has the knowledge and tools to navigate the world confidently and responsibly.

Neglecting to fix problems- Many parents endure months or even years of frustration because they believe certain problems are unsolvable or they simply accept them. Common issues like bedtime battles, frequent night waking, temper tantrums, or behavioral problems in older children can seem overwhelming. However, most of these problems can be worked through and resolved with effort and consistency. While it may take time and patience, many parenting challenges are not permanent and can be improved. Seeking help is a smart move—whether it's reading books, visiting websites, or reaching out to experts and fellow parents. Though your child didn't come with a manual, there is a wealth of resources available to guide you through these challenges. The key to successful parenting is maintaining patience and staying positive at every stage. With the right approach and mindset, you can work through difficulties and foster a healthier, more positive relationship with your child.

Overestimating or underestimating problems- Before attempting to fix any issues, it's crucial to first assess what is and isn't truly a problem. Unfortunately, parents sometimes either overestimate or underestimate the problems they are facing with their children. Parents who underestimate problems may miss critical signs, such as a child struggling with depression or substance use, which could go unnoticed and untreated. On the other hand, overestimating problems often stems from anxiety, which can result in children feeling smothered or overly controlled by their parents. When parents underestimate issues, they risk invalidating their child's emotions, which can lead to the child feeling misunderstood or unsupported. This might unintentionally teach the child to avoid confronting or discussing problems. On the other hand, overestimating issues can create unnecessary stress and pressure, making the child feel overwhelmed. It's important to strike a balance—acknowledging and addressing problems when they arise, while also giving children the space to grow and navigate challenges independently. Understanding and accurately assessing the situation allows for more effective and supportive parenting.

Having unrealistic expectations- Having unrealistic expectations for your children can lead to unnecessary stress and problems. This often happens when parents become frustrated with milestones that aren't being met as quickly as expected, such as a toddler who isn't potty trained yet, a six-year-old who is still wetting the bed, or a moody child. It's essential that your expectations align with your child's developmental stage and abilities. When parents impose unrealistic standards, it creates pressure for the child to be "perfect," which can have negative effects on their mental health. Children naturally want to feel accepted, especially by their parents, and if they feel they are disappointing them by not meeting these high expectations, it can lead to stress, anxiety, and a lack of self-esteem. Some experts suggest that when children can't meet these unrealistic demands, they may seek validation through negative behaviors. Over time, this can result in feelings of shame and the belief that they are "not good enough." This cycle of unmet expectations can even contribute to anxiety and a diminished sense of self-worth. To foster a healthy emotional environment, it's important to set realistic, age-appropriate expectations for your child and offer support and encouragement rather than focusing on perfection.

Being inconsistent- Few things can harm your children more than an inconsistent parenting style. If you are sometimes very strict but other times give in or appear indifferent to your child's behavior, they will struggle to understand what is expected of them and how to act. Experts emphasize that inconsistency in parenting or discipline creates confusion and mixed signals for children. When parents fail to follow through on rules or consequences, children may not take their authority seriously, which can lead to a lack of respect. Additionally, inconsistency can make children feel anxious and uncertain, as they may not know what to expect from their parents in any given situation. For children to feel secure and understand boundaries, it's important for parents to maintain consistency in their approach. Clear, consistent expectations help children develop a sense of trust, respect, and emotional stability.

Avoiding rules or limits- You may think you're doing your kids a favour by letting them do whatever they want, but most children, especially younger ones, find it difficult to function without clear guidelines. Having rules, setting limits, following consistent routines, and offering limited choices help children understand what to expect throughout the day. Experts agree that when parents fail to set rules or establish boundaries, the risks include negative behaviors such as temper tantrums, hostility, defiance, and attention-seeking behaviors. These behaviors not only affect children in the short term but also impact how they respond to situations in the long term. In the short term, children may overstep boundaries and show little respect for their parents. In the long term, they may develop a sense of entitlement, expecting to get what they want even when their behavior is poor. Establishing rules and boundaries helps children understand limits, fosters respect, and teaches them how to behave appropriately in different situations.

Fighting back- Fighting with your child doesn't always mean physical confrontation. It can also involve getting angry, yelling, or repeating yourself repeatedly. Arguing or fighting with your kids gives them negative attention and can give them a sense of power over you, as they trigger such strong reactions. Instead of stopping the problematic behavior, fighting back often unintentionally rewards it. This can reinforce the behavior you're trying to correct. Rather than engaging in power struggles, it's more effective to use alternative discipline techniques, such as time-outs or logical and natural consequences. The key is to avoid wasting time fighting. By staying calm and consistent, and using well-thought-out strategies, you can guide your child's behavior more effectively without giving in to the urge to argue or escalate the situation.

Neglecting to change what doesn't work- Not recognizing or adjusting parenting techniques that aren't working can be just as problematic as not addressing the issues at all. For example, you might think that time-outs are an effective form of discipline, but if you find yourself using them every day to correct the same behavior, it may not be effective for your child. Similarly, if your bedtime routine involves your child repeatedly getting out of bed, causing the process to stretch on for an hour and leaving both of you frustrated, it's a sign that you may need to find a new approach. If what you're trying isn't yielding positive results, it's important to acknowledge that a change is needed. Don't hesitate to seek professional advice or explore alternative strategies. Parenting can be challenging, and seeking guidance when you're unsure can help you find more effective ways to manage behaviors and create a more positive environment for both you and your child.

Failing to lead by example- Children often look to the models in their environment to understand what is acceptable and what isn't, and since parents are the most influential figures in their lives, leading by example is crucial. When parents model positive behaviors, children learn valuable life skills. For instance, it's beneficial for kids to witness healthy communication and conflict resolution skills in action. Experts agree that when parents exhibit positive and healthy behaviors, children learn how to handle challenges or stressful situations with effective coping strategies. Additionally, children develop positive interpersonal skills and learn how to interact with others in a respectful and constructive manner. By being a good role model, parents set the foundation for their children to develop strong emotional intelligence, social skills, and resilience, which are essential for navigating life's challenges.

Fighting your child's battle- While there are situations where parents should step in to help their child navigate conflict, constantly fighting their battles for them prevents kids from learning how to interact with others and resolve issues independently. With younger children, parents can model how to handle conflict and assert themselves. However, as children grow older, it's important for parents to gradually encourage them to take on more responsibility in resolving conflicts on their own. Experts agree that when parents consistently fight their children's battles, it teaches the child that they don't have a voice. Instead, children should be encouraged to express themselves assertively and in a positive way. This approach helps children develop the skills needed to establish healthy boundaries with others, fostering independence, confidence, and the ability to handle future conflicts constructively.

Rescuing your children before they make mistakes -It's natural for parents to want to protect their children from the pain of making mistakes, but mistakes are essential for growth and learning. They provide an opportunity to reflect on actions, understand what went wrong, and figure out how to do better in the future. By making mistakes, children learn responsibility and resilience. Experts emphasize that constantly rescuing your children from mistakes prevents them from experiencing this learning process. It can also lead to unhealthy beliefs about themselves, as they may start to feel incapable or inadequate when faced with challenges. This pattern can hinder their development of emotional resilience, self-soothing skills, and problem-solving abilities. Furthermore, if children are shielded from failure, they may develop a fear of failure, struggle with low self-confidence, and lack the courage to try new things. Allowing children to make mistakes and guiding them through the learning process helps them build confidence, learn from their experiences, and develop the emotional strength needed to face challenges in the future.

Failing to listen to your child- When you listen to your child, you're not only acknowledging their thoughts and feelings, but you're also validating their emotions. This act of listening communicates to your child that they are important to you, which strengthens the bond between you. When parents fail to listen, however, children may feel dismissed or unimportant. Over time, this lack of validation can lead to issues with self-esteem, as children may internalize the belief that they are not worthy of attention or approval. As they grow, they may carry the weight of constantly feeling like a disappointment, which can affect their confidence and emotional well-being. By taking the time to listen to your child, you help them feel heard, valued, and respected. This builds a foundation of trust and encourages open communication, fostering a positive environment where they can freely express themselves without fear of judgment.

Harsh Effects of Electronic Gadgets on our Kids

Technology has become an integral part of our everyday existence, with devices such as computers, smart phones, and various gadgets shaping how we live, work, and play. These tools are popular not only among adults but also increasingly so among children. In today's world, it is almost impossible to completely keep children away from these devices. However, the growing prevalence of gadgets has led to a concerning trend—technology addiction among the younger generation.

Research reveals that children spend a significant amount of time using gadgets such as phones, gaming consoles, televisions, and music players. They engage in activities like gaming, video streaming, chatting, and browsing, often neglecting important aspects such as proper posture, screen brightness, and maintaining a safe distance from screens. Prolonged screen exposure can strain their eyes and impact their overall health.

Continuous screen time can cause discomfort and lead to problems such as eye irritation and difficulty focusing. If adults find it challenging to manage prolonged exposure, imagine the strain on a child's developing eyes. While technology cannot be entirely eliminated from our lives, steps can be taken to reduce its negative impact on children. Alarmingly, studies show that even toddlers, some as young as two years old, can operate devices with ease—an ability they develop as naturally as using a feeding bottle. In the U.S., studies have revealed that one in three children can use a tablet or Smartphone before they can even speak.

Adverse Effects of Gadgets on Children

Brain Development- During early childhood, the brain undergoes rapid growth, tripling in size and continuing to develop into adulthood. Excessive gadget use can hinder this development, leading to issues such as attention deficits, cognitive delays, impaired learning, impulsivity, and difficulty with self-regulation. Experts recommend that parents prioritize interactive activities like reading, singing, and talking with their children over screen time.

Obesity- Sedentary activities such as gaming and watching videos contribute to obesity in children. Surveys indicate that one in three U.S. children is overweight, which increases the risk of diabetes, heart disease, and other health complications. Encouraging outdoor play and physical activities helps children stay active, burn calories, and build social connections.

Aggressive Behavior- Exposure to violent games and prolonged screen time can lead to aggression and behavioral issues. Tantrums are common among younger children, while older ones may exhibit defiance. Instead of relying on gadgets to pacify children, parents can engage them with creative toys, books, or interactive play.

Radiation Risks- Wireless devices emit radiation, classified as a potential health risk by the World Health Organization.

Reduced Social Interaction- Overuse of gadgets can hinder a child's communication skills and disrupt their ability to interact with others. In family settings, children immersed in screens miss opportunities to bond with parents and siblings.

Sleep Disruption- Addiction to gadgets often leads to sleep deprivation, as children prioritize screen time over rest. Over time, this habit can negatively affect their mood and behavior.

Limited Exposure to Nature- Gadgets keep children indoors, preventing them from exploring the natural world. Outdoor activities like running, playing, and interacting with peers are essential for their physical and emotional growth.

Vision Problems- Prolonged screen exposure strains the eyes and can lead to vision problems such as myopia. Research suggests that focusing on objects at varying distances, especially in outdoor environments, supports healthy eye development.

Addiction- Unchecked gadget use fosters dependency, limiting children's exposure to activities that promote holistic growth. Parents should encourage hobbies and interactions that nurture mental, physical, and emotional well-being.

Mental Health Concerns- Excessive screen time has been linked to childhood depression and anxiety. A lack of real-world engagement can amplify feelings of isolation and loneliness.

Speech and Language Delays- Children learn to communicate through interaction. Over-reliance on screens reduces opportunities for verbal exchanges, which are critical for developing speech and language skills. Studies show that increased screen time correlates with delayed speech in young children.

Strategies for Managing Technology Use

Although technology has its drawbacks, it can be a valuable tool when used wisely. Parents can adopt several strategies to minimize the negative effects of gadgets:

Set Limits: Establish clear boundaries for screen time and encourage breaks after 30-40 minutes of device use.

Encourage Outdoor Play: Promote physical activities and exposure to nature to support overall well-being.

Create a Comfortable Setup: Ensure that devices are used at an ergonomic workstation tailored to the child's height.

Prioritize Sleep: Avoid using gadgets at least an hour before bedtime to improve sleep quality.

Promote Social Interaction: Encourage face-to-face communication to develop social skills and emotional intelligence.

By fostering balanced habits, parents can ensure that technology serves as a helpful resource rather than a hindrance. The key lies in guiding children to use devices responsibly while prioritizing activities that nurture their growth and development.

How to Safe Guard your Kids from Influence of Wrong People?

Every parent wants to raise their children to be kind, compassionate, and decent human beings. However, this is not an easy task. As kids grow, they encounter people with varying values—some may serve as good role models, while others could have a negative influence. It's impossible to know for sure when meeting someone for the first time. Parenthood involves gradually letting go as your child matures and becomes more independent, but the world is full of dangers, from harmful objects to toxic people. While you can't guarantee their safety at all times, you can teach your children key safety measures, build their self-esteem and judgment, and maintain open, honest communication. Empowering your child with these tools will help them navigate potentially threatening situations when you're not there to protect them.

Holidays, often associated with family and friends, can bring joy and connection, but they may also expose children to dysfunctional or harmful individuals. Experts emphasize the importance of shielding kids from toxic people. Setting firm boundaries with such family members teaches children they deserve healthy relationships and that their concerns matter. If a family member only accepts a child when they hide parts of themselves, that person should not have access to the child. Toxicity can be difficult to identify, especially if you grew up in a similar environment. Signs include controlling behavior, ridicule, gas lighting, abuse (verbal, emotional, physical, or sexual), or making racist, sexist, or other discriminatory remarks. Such behaviors harm children's mental health, a vital component of their overall well-being. Toxic stress can derail healthy development, affecting learning, behavior, and health for a lifetime. Children notice and absorb these dynamics, and how you respond will leave a lasting impression.

Friends also play a significant role in shaping your child. Pay attention to how your child behaves around their friends and look for changes in their demeanour. Negative influences might manifest in behaviors like imitating poor attitudes, fear of disappointing friends, or associating with rule-breakers or risk-takers. Peer pressure can lead to risky behaviors, including substance use. If you notice signs of trouble, consult a physician or professional promptly.

To guide your child through these challenges

Teach the Power of "No" – Empower your child to trust their instincts and speak up if they feel uncomfortable or scared around someone.

Clarify Boundaries – Teach children that no one should invade their personal space or force them into situations without your consent.

Designate Trusted Adults – Identify safe adults who can care for your child in your absence and ensure your child knows not to deviate from this list.

Explain Safety Rules – Stress that they should never get into a car or go anywhere with someone without your permission. Teach them to scream, run, and fight back if someone tries to harm them.

Avoid Instilling Fear – Focus on building confidence and teaching them how to handle dangers instead of making them fearful of every situation.

Practice Safety Scenarios – Regularly discuss what they would do in case of separation or danger and identify safe spaces and people to seek help from.

When it comes to online safety, explore sites, apps, and games together before allowing your child to use them. Supervise their online activities, set limits, and use parental controls. Encourage open communication so they feel comfortable sharing concerns. Be an active listener, offering reassurance and guidance.

If your child's friends seem like a bad influence, address it calmly. Criticizing their friends directly may lead to defensiveness. Instead, cite specific examples of negative behavior, such as disrespect, and explain your concerns objectively. Set limits on their interactions with these friends, aligning the rules with your family values.

Lastly, carve out time for one-on-one moments with your child, even during busy family gatherings. A simple 15–30 minutes daily can provide an opportunity to address challenges, answer questions, and strengthen your bond. By maintaining open communication, setting boundaries, and teaching life skills, you can help your child navigate the complexities of growing up with confidence and resilience.

Teaching Manners

Teaching children manners is essential for their personal and social development. It's never too early to start, as these lessons provide the foundation for healthy interactions and future success. Without proper manners, children may struggle to communicate effectively and could face isolation, negatively impacting their social and work lives as they grow older. Starting early helps children develop these skills over time, enabling them to thrive as they mature.

For preschoolers, teaching manners can be engaging and fun. Children are naturally curious and eager to learn, often imitating the actions of adults. This is an ideal time to introduce basic manners such as greetings and self-introductions. At this age, they are learning to interact and make friends, and polite communication helps them build meaningful connections. Respect is another critical lesson to teach early. Children should learn to treat others as they want to be treated. Key concepts include using "please," "thank you," and "I'm sorry," as well as practicing active listening and showing consideration for others.

Good manners have numerous benefits, including increased confidence, higher self-esteem, empathy, and better social skills. Teaching these habits helps children become considerate adults who are better equipped to navigate social and professional settings. Parents and educators play a crucial role in this process by setting clear behavioral expectations and serving as role models. Children learn by observing adults, so consistently demonstrating polite behavior, such as speaking kindly and following rules, reinforces these lessons.

Tailoring expectations to a child's developmental stage is essential. For toddlers, start with simple gestures like saying "please" and "thank you" or waiting their turn. Older children can handle more advanced skills, such as proper introductions and being considerate guests. Teenagers should learn complex manners like phone etiquette and effective communication. As children grow, it's important to periodically review and build on these lessons.

When teaching manners, focus on one skill at a time to avoid overwhelming your child. Practice regularly through real-life situations and role-playing, which provide a safe space to explore different scenarios. For instance, you can rehearse how to thank someone for a gift or how to include everyone in a game. Praise your child when they display good manners, as positive reinforcement encourages continued effort.

Mistakes are part of the learning process. If your child forgets their manners, offer gentle reminders and give them opportunities to correct their behavior. Avoid harsh criticism, which can discourage them. Instead, explain why certain behaviors matter and how they can improve. For example, remind them that chewing with their mouth closed is polite because it's unpleasant for others to see otherwise.

When children repeatedly ignore expectations, consequences may be necessary. Ensure these consequences are directly related to the behavior. For instance, ending a playmate if they are rude to a friend or temporarily taking away a toy if they refuse to pick up after themselves. Consistency in enforcing consequences reinforces the importance of good manners.

Ultimately, teaching manners takes time, patience, and consistent effort. By modelling the desired behaviors, offering praise, and providing opportunities to practice, you help your child develop habits that will serve them well throughout their lives. Good manners are more than just polite gestures—they are tools for building positive relationships and thriving in society.

How to Motivate and Inspire your Child to Find Passion?

Learning is an essential process that shapes a child's ability to become an effective and extraordinary individual. When parents nurture a love for learning early in a child's life, it builds concentration, expands knowledge, and equips them to achieve their future goals. Motivation, the driving force behind behavior, plays a crucial role in this journey.

Motivation in children can be categorized as intrinsic or extrinsic:

Intrinsic Motivation: Engaging in activities for the joy and satisfaction they bring.

Extrinsic Motivation: Performing tasks for external rewards or outcomes.

While both types can influence behavior, intrinsic motivation leads to higher engagement and better results. For instance, a study at the University of Rochester found that students who enjoyed reading an article performed better in recalling and understanding it compared to those who didn't, even after accounting for differences in aptitude.

Challenges with Extrinsic Motivation

Parents often use the **"carrot and stick"** approach—rewards and punishments—to encourage desired behaviors. While this may yield quick results, it often reduces intrinsic motivation over time. Once the external incentives are removed, the behavior may stop.

Encouraging Intrinsic Motivation

Building intrinsic motivation in children requires thoughtful strategies:

Make Learning Enjoyable:

Avoid controlling methods like nagging, scolding, or excessive rewards.

Create an environment where learning is fun and fulfilling, not just about completing tasks.

Encourage curiosity by linking new subjects to real-life applications.

Promote Autonomy:

Let children make their own choices within safe boundaries.

Allow them to experience the consequences of their decisions to foster responsibility.

Help Internalize the Importance:

Teach children the value and meaning behind activities, especially those they find less enjoyable.

Explain why certain tasks matter and how they contribute to long-term goals.

Set Optimal Challenges:

Offer tasks that are slightly more difficult than what the child has mastered to encourage growth without discouragement.

Foster a growth mindset by emphasizing effort and practice over innate ability.

Build Relatedness:

Strengthen emotional bonds through authoritative parenting—being warm, supportive, and setting clear boundaries.

Get involved in your child's activities, whether it's helping with homework, coaching sports, or volunteering in their school.

Practical Tips for Motivation

Set Goals: Simple, achievable goals give children a sense of purpose and direction.

Encourage Planning: Help children plan activities, teaching them logical thinking and organization.

Provide Meaningful Rewards: Instead of tangible rewards like toys or treats, focus on intrinsic rewards like a sense of accomplishment or quality time with family.

Inspire Through Example: Be a role model for the behaviors and values you want your child to adopt.

Celebrate Effort and Success: Acknowledge your child's efforts, progress, and achievements with specific and genuine praise.

Storytelling for Motivation

Inspirational stories can teach children valuable life lessons. Use moral tales, biographies, or mythological stories to convey important messages. Make storytelling engaging by using different voices, asking questions, and involving children in creative activities like skits based on the stories.

Encouragement and Support

Encouragement is a powerful motivator. It helps children persist through failures and boosts their confidence. Avoid being overly judgmental, and focus on their efforts rather than outcomes. Teach them to embrace their unique qualities and view challenges as opportunities for growth.

Seeing the Bigger Picture

Help children understand how small tasks contribute to larger goals. For instance, explain how studying now can open doors to exciting careers in the future.

By fostering intrinsic motivation and creating a supportive environment, parents can help children develop a lifelong love for learning and equip them with the skills to achieve their dreams.

Developing your Child's Self-Esteem

Self-esteem is a child's sense of self-worth and confidence in their abilities. It significantly influences how they perceive themselves and interact with the world.

Characteristics of Self-Esteem:

Kids with High Self-Esteem:

Feel liked and accepted.

Display confidence in their abilities.

Take pride in their achievements.

Believe in themselves and their potential.

Think positively about themselves.

Kids with Low Self-Esteem:

Are overly critical of themselves.

Feel inferior to peers.

Focus on failures rather than successes.

Lack confidence and self-belief.

Struggle to cope with mistakes or setbacks.

Impact of Self-Esteem:

Children with healthy self-esteem are more willing to try new things, persist after failures, and succeed academically and socially. Conversely, those with low self-esteem may withdraw, struggle with challenges, and perform below their potential.

How to Build Self-Esteem:

Teach kids new skills patiently, offering guidance and encouragement.

Praise their efforts and accomplishments thoughtfully.

Be a positive role model.

Avoid harsh criticism; focus on strengths.

Encourage participation in household responsibilities.

Share personal challenges and seek their opinions, fostering mutual respect.

Making your kids wiser and smart

As parents, we naturally want our children to excel in school, stay out of trouble, and grow into successful adults. However, it's important to understand that a child's brain is not just a smaller version of an adult brain. It is a developing organ that adapts and wires itself based on its environment. This means parents play a crucial role in shaping both the physical and social worlds their child experiences, as these environments provide the "wiring instructions" for their brain's development.

Raising an intelligent child comes with unique challenges and opportunities. At first, it may seem like fostering intellectual growth and curiosity requires significant time and effort. While this is true, the rewards are immense—a stronger bond with your child and a deeper understanding of their abilities. By nurturing their intelligence and encouraging curiosity, you can help them thrive in an increasingly competitive world.

In today's fast-paced society, many parents worry about whether their child is intelligent enough and wonder if there are ways to support their cognitive development. **Research suggests that the right amount of stimulation during the early years can significantly enhance a child's abilities.** These formative years are, therefore, the ideal time to focus on intellectual growth, setting the foundation for a lifetime of learning and success.

Think of parenting as being a gardener, not a carpenter. While carpenters shape wood into specific forms, gardeners nurture growth by creating a fertile and supportive environment. Similarly, parents can either try to meld their child into something specific, like a concert violinist, or they can provide an environment that allows the child to grow naturally in their own unique direction.

For instance, you may dream of your child playing a symphony on the violin one day. However, forcing them to take lessons when they don't enjoy music could lead to frustration. A gardener's approach would be to introduce a variety of musical experiences—perhaps letting them explore instruments, listen to different genres, or even bang on pots and pans. This way, you can observe what sparks their interest and nurture their natural inclinations.

Once you understand your child's unique traits and interests—like discovering what type of "plant" they are—you can create the right environment to help them take root and thrive.

Talk and read to your child often. Studies show that even when children are only a few months old and cannot yet understand the meaning of words, their brains still process and benefit from hearing them. This exposure helps build the neural foundation for later learning. The more words a child hears, the stronger this foundation becomes, leading to a larger vocabulary and better reading comprehension as they grow.

Teaching emotional vocabulary is particularly beneficial. By introducing words that describe feelings, you help your child understand and navigate social interactions with greater flexibility. Take time to elaborate on emotions during everyday interactions. For example, if you see a crying child, you might say, "That boy is feeling sad because he's in pain. He might want a hug from his parents to feel better."

Think of yourself as a tour guide, helping your child explore the mysterious world of human emotions, movements, and sounds. By talking about the causes and effects of emotions, you not only enrich their understanding but also foster empathy and emotional intelligence.

Answering your child's endless "why" questions can be exhausting, but it's an essential part of their learning process. When you take the time to explain things, you help them make sense of the world by turning something unfamiliar into something predictable. A brain that can predict outcomes works more efficiently and effectively.

Avoid responding with "Because I said so." Instead, provide clear reasons for why certain behaviors are expected. Children who understand the reasons behind rules are better equipped to regulate their actions. For example, if a child is told not to eat all the cookies, simply saying, "Don't do it because I said so," may only work when an authority figure is present. However, explaining the reasoning— "If you eat all the cookies, you might get a stomachache, and your siblings will be upset they didn't get dessert"—teaches them to think about the consequences of their actions.

This approach not only helps them understand cause and effect but also fosters empathy by encouraging them to consider how their behavior impacts others. Over time, these explanations build a foundation for thoughtful decision-making and emotional intelligence.

When your child misbehaves, focus on describing the behavior rather than labelling the person. For example, if your son hits his sister, avoid calling him a "bad boy." Instead, be specific: "Stop hitting your sister—it hurts her and makes her feel upset. Please tell her you're sorry." This approach addresses the behavior while encouraging empathy and accountability.

The same principle applies to praise. Instead of saying, "You're a good girl," acknowledge specific actions: "You made a great choice not to hit your brother back." This kind of feedback helps children form meaningful concepts about their actions and how they define themselves, reinforcing positive behaviors.

When discussing behaviors, even with storybook characters, describe the action rather than labelling the person. For instance, instead of saying, "Raja is a liar," say, "Raja told a lie." Then, engage your child with questions like, "Why do you think Raja did that? How would others feel if they found out? Should they forgive Raja?" This approach fosters curiosity and critical thinking rather than judgment.

By focusing on actions and exploring motivations, you model flexibility and empathy. Children learn that behaviors can change and that being honest or kind is about making thoughtful choices in specific situations, not fixed traits.

Encourage children to imitate you. Have you noticed how tasks that feel like work to you, such as cleaning the house or gardening, can seem like play to a child? This is because children learn best by watching, playing, and, most importantly, copying adults. It's an efficient way for them to acquire new skills while also gaining a sense of accomplishment.

To make the most of this natural tendency, involve your child in your activities. Hand them a child-sized broom, a toy garden spade, or a pretend tool that matches what you're using. Then, invite them to join in. This simple act turns everyday tasks into valuable learning experiences while also strengthening your bond with them. Let the imitation begin, and watch their confidence and skills grow!

Expose your child to a variety of people in safe and positive environments. Along with familiar family members like grandparents, aunts, uncles, and friends, try to introduce them to a wide range of individuals, including children from diverse backgrounds. The more diversity they encounter, the better.

Research has shown that babies who interact regularly with speakers of different languages develop critical brain pathways that help them learn other languages later in life. Similarly, babies who are exposed to a range of faces and people develop the ability to distinguish and remember a greater variety of faces, which can foster a deeper understanding of diversity.

This early exposure can be one of the simplest yet most powerful ways to promote inclusivity and anti-racism as a parent, helping your child grow up with a more open, accepting, and empathetic view of the world.

Encourage your child's sense of agency by applauding their efforts to try things on their own, whether it's getting dressed or solving a puzzle. This is an important part of their development. Even actions that may seem like misbehavior, such as a toddler throwing their toys on the floor and waiting for you to pick them up, are often an attempt to understand how their actions affect the world. For example, a two-year-old may not be trying to manipulate you but instead experimenting with the physics of gravity.

Allow them the space to explore and learn from their actions. If they drop their toys, let them try again. Knowing when to step in and when to let them struggle can be challenging, but it's important for their growth. If you're always there to guide them and take care of every need, they may not learn to do things for themselves. Sometimes, allowing your child to struggle helps build resilience and teaches them the consequences of their actions. This is a crucial step in fostering independence and problem-solving skills.

Research suggests that music lessons can enhance a child's cognitive abilities. Studies show that children who receive music lessons tend to exhibit greater increases in full-scale IQ compared to children in control groups. While the effect is relatively small, it is consistent across various IQ subtests, including verbal and performance scales, as well as standardized measures of academic achievement. These findings suggest that music education may contribute to broader cognitive development, although the impact may vary depending on individual circumstances and the extent of musical training.

Sleep deprivation can significantly affect a child's cognitive performance. Losing one hour of sleep can equate to a loss of two years in cognitive maturation and development. This highlights the crucial role that sleep plays in children's ability to learn, think, and perform academically. Ensuring children get enough sleep is essential for their overall cognitive and emotional well-being.

Teaching Values and Ethics to your Kids

Values are the fundamental beliefs that inspire children to act, while ethics guide them in distinguishing right from wrong. Together, they shape a child's character, preparing them to navigate life's challenges with integrity and compassion. Parents, teachers, and society collectively play a pivotal role in instilling these principles, especially during early childhood when children are most impressionable.

Why Teach Values and Ethics Early?

Foundation for Character: Early lessons in values and ethics shape a child's behavior, decision-making, and interpersonal relationships throughout life.

Guidance in a Changing World: In today's rapidly evolving world, values provide stability and direction, empowering children to positively influence their surroundings.

Social Acceptance and Respect: A strong moral foundation helps children grow into individuals who are admired and respected by society.

Core Values and Ethics for Children

Respect and Self-Respect:

Teach children to honour diverse opinions and respond politely, even when they disagree.

Self-respect enables them to set boundaries and stand up for themselves without fear.

Hard Work and Strong Work Ethic:

Emphasize the importance of effort over shortcuts. Encourage children to see hard work as an opportunity, not a burden.

Gratitude:

Foster appreciation for what they have and discourage entitlement. Teach them to express thankfulness regularly.

Generosity and Helping Others:

Model generosity through actions, like sharing or helping neighbours. Encourage children to donate toys, clothes, or time to those in need.

Honesty:

Highlight the long-term benefits of truthfulness over short-term gains from dishonesty.

Empathy:

Help children understand others' feelings and perspectives by discussing real-life scenarios or storybook characters. Including about both hero and villain perspectives to teach why and what is the difference, and conclude it with real life scenarios so they can understand it better and apply in real life.

Cooperation:

Promote teamwork through family activities and household chores.

Justice:

Teach fairness and equality by setting consistent rules and explaining their rationale.

Courage:

Celebrate acts of bravery, such as standing up against bullying or admitting mistakes.

Acceptance:

Encourage children to appreciate differences in opinions, cultures, and lifestyles.

Responsibility:

Assign age-appropriate tasks and praise their efforts to build accountability.

Perseverance:

Instill a "never give up" attitude by encouraging them to overcome challenges.

Self-Control:

Teach patience and emotional regulation by modelling calm behavior in stressful situations.

Family Values:

Emphasize the importance of family bonds and support, creating a sense of belonging.

Adjusting and Compromising:

Help children understand the value of flexibility while ensuring they don't compromise their core values or identity.

Respect for Religion:

Teach children to honour their own faith while respecting others' beliefs and practices.

Methods to Teach Values and Ethics

Be a Role Model:

Children learn by observing parents and teachers. Demonstrate the values you wish to instill. Simple acts like saying "please" and "thank you" reinforce good manners.

Teach Good Manners:

Start early by using polite phrases and modelling considerate behavior.

Use Stories and Examples:

Narrate stories with moral lessons or discuss real-life events to illustrate ethical principles. Especially about great personalities, and from books such as Panchatantra, stories of Tenali Rama, Akbar and Birbal, etc.

Encourage Independent Thinking:

Discuss consequences of actions and encourage children to reflect on their decisions. Allow them to guess and present their views on random situations whether it can be a plot of a story, or a nearby situation and then discuss with them.

Praise and Correct Wisely:

Recognize good behavior and correct mistakes constructively, focusing on actions rather than labelling the child.

Promote Community Involvement:

Encourage volunteering or participating in community service to develop a sense of responsibility and empathy.

By teaching children values and ethics early, parents and educators lay the groundwork for their growth into compassionate, responsible, and resilient individuals. These principles not only guide children in making better decisions but also empower them to contribute positively to society.

According to research, from ages 0 to 7, children go through their "programming years". During this time, their brains are mostly function in Alpha and Theta states, similar to hypnosis or meditation. This makes them highly receptive to their environment and open to learning and suggestions. These early years shape their beliefs about themselves and the world, many of which remain unconscious but influence their behaviour, goals, relationships, and achievements throughout life. Essentially, most beliefs we hold were shaped or suggested by others, especially during this critical period. Now you, as a parent, you will play a crucial role in these programming years of your children.

Between birth and 2 years old, the human brain functions primarily in the lowest brain-wave cycle, that is 0.5 to 4 cycles per second. These are called Delta waves. Adults in deep sleep are in delta and this explains why a newborn usually can't stay awake for long. Even as they grow, their subconscious mind still dominates, with little critical thinking. In this state, babies learn basic behaviours, like copying smiles, which helps them connect with caregivers and adapt to their environment.

The Theta wave frequencies measure 4 to 8 cycles per second and are predominant in children aged between 2 and 6. Children operating in Theta are very connected to their internal world. They live in the realm of imagination, and daydreaming, and are still not able to show signs of critical, rational thinking. This is a super learning state, where the child is open to suggestions. These children are likely to accept what you tell them as true. People in hypnosis and animals are also in this frequency.

Between ages 5 to 8, the brain waves have changed into an Alpha frequency, 8 to 13 cycles per second. This is the point at which the analytical mind begins to form. Children start to interpret and draw conclusions from their environment. Still, though, the inner world of imagination tends to be as real as the outer world of reality. Children in this age-group tend to have a foot in both worlds, using both left and right brain hemispheres at the same time. People who meditate or who are in a light trance are in this frequency, which is peaceful and relaxed, though alert with powerful ideas and inspiration. **This is a great state to be in when brain storming, creating ideas or**

learning. (Schools should take note - kids learn when they are relaxed and having fun, not when they are stressed).

From ages 8 to 12 and onwards, brain activity increases to anything above 13 cycles per second. This is the world of conscious, analytical thinking. The mind is awake, focused, and alert and is capable of logical thinking. Adults spend most of their time in this cycle.

So, from above information we can conclude that parenting during early childhood determines the person's life goals, interests, relationships and identity. Hence, it's crucial for you to focus on parenting them, who knows, may be the next great personality, in front of you.

Happy parenting!!!

PART 3

PARENTING TEENAGER

Social Emotional development in Teenagers

Emotional development during adolescence

Adolescence is a dynamic phase of life marked by significant emotional, behavioral, and cognitive changes. These changes are influenced by a combination of shifting environments, stressors, and developmental processes at both psychological and neurobiological levels. This period typically begins with the onset of puberty and concludes as young individuals take on adult roles. Adolescence encompasses a wide range of transformations across physical, social, cognitive, and emotional domains.

Research indicates that adolescents often experience heightened emotions, both positive and negative, and face a higher risk of mental health challenges tied to difficulties with emotional regulation. Compared to children and adults, adolescents' emotions tend to be more intense and variable.

Social dynamics also evolve during this stage, as peer groups expand and become more complex. Adolescents navigate fluctuations in social affiliation and status, while concerns about social evaluation grow. As they spend more time with peers and less with family, they begin making independent decisions with limited experience. This newfound independence, combined with inexperience, can feel overwhelming as these decisions often have significant consequences for their education and future careers.

Physically, adolescence is characterized by rapid growth, hormonal changes, and shifts in sleep patterns, which often conflict with societal demands. Healthy emotional development during this time involves gradually improving the ability to recognize, evaluate, and manage emotions. This process is influenced by biological changes as well as environmental and contextual factors.

Adolescents typically become more attuned to their own emotions and the emotions of others, though this awareness is still developing. Adults often expect teens to manage their emotions effectively in academic, social, and other settings, but this can be challenging in the face of a complex environment. Some adolescents may embrace new challenges as they gain independence, while others may need extra support to build their confidence. Emotional development during adolescence offers opportunities for young people to develop strengths, refine skills, and discover their unique qualities, all of which contribute to overall well-being.

Emotional Development by Age

Ages 11-12:

At this stage, early puberty brings physical changes that can make preteens feel awkward or self-conscious. They may focus more on themselves and compare themselves to peers. Their thinking tends to be concrete, focusing on the present rather than long-term consequences. Common concerns include managing rapid physical changes and fitting in with friends. Parents can help by addressing their child's self-consciousness and providing reassurance that these changes are normal. Sharing personal experiences from their own adolescence can also help preteens feel understood. If concerns persist, seeking guidance from a counsellor or health professional may be beneficial.

Ages 13-14:

Teens in this age group often become more sensitive to social pressures and exclusion. This sensitivity may manifest in behaviors like slamming doors, seeking privacy, or distancing themselves from adults. While these behaviors may seem unsettling, they reflect a natural need for independence. Parents can support their teens by actively listening to their concerns, helping them navigate peer dynamics, and modelling healthy relationships. While teens may prioritize time with peers, family support remains a crucial buffer against emotional challenges.

Ages 15-16:

Teens at this stage may engage in thrill-seeking behaviors, such as experimenting with alcohol, drugs, or sexual activity. They may also experience stress related to academic performance, relationships, and self-image. This period is marked by emotional fluctuations, with teens oscillating between confidence and self-doubt. As they transition from concrete to abstract thinking, they begin to understand the long-term consequences of their actions. Parents should maintain open communication, set clear boundaries, and encourage their teens to develop problem-solving skills. Close parent-teen relationships can reduce the likelihood of risky behaviors.

Ages 17-21:

By this stage, most teens have reached physical maturity and are better equipped to regulate their emotions and plan for the future. Individual relationships often take precedence over peer groups, and teens may prioritize goals like college or career preparation. However, some may still engage in risky behaviors, such as binge drinking or unprotected sex. It's important to remember that the brain continues to develop into the mid-20s, and parental guidance remains vital. Parents should encourage responsible decision-making, provide tools for navigating challenges, and create opportunities for teens to learn from mistakes while offering support when needed.

Adolescence is a time of intense emotional growth, marked by highs and lows. Parents play a critical role in helping teens navigate this journey by offering guidance, support, and understanding. By recognizing what teens experience emotionally, parents can better equip them to become emotionally resilient and healthy adults.

Bonding with your Teen

The teenage years are often seen as a confusing and challenging time for both children and parents. Yet, they are also critical years for shaping a young person's character and future. As teens explore their identity and test boundaries, parents may feel frustrated, fearing they are losing the close bond they once shared. However, with patience, understanding, and love, this phase can become an opportunity to foster a deeper connection and mutual respect. Here's how:

1. Listen Actively

Pay attention to what your teen says, both verbally and non-verbally. Teens often communicate more through their tone, body language, and what they leave unsaid. Being an attentive listener shows that you value their thoughts and feelings.

2. Create Rituals for Connection

Small, consistent acts—like sharing a daily coffee or a hug before they leave—help establish reliable moments of connection. These rituals become comforting anchors in your relationship.

3. Be a Sounding Board

Rather than solving their problems, let your teen share their challenges while you listen and ask thoughtful questions. This helps them feel supported and empowered to make their own decisions.

4. Acknowledge Their Efforts

Teens often feel overwhelmed by schoolwork and other responsibilities. Show empathy by appreciating their hard work. Simple gestures like offering to review an essay or bringing snacks during study time can make them feel cared for.

5. Show Genuine Interest

Ask specific questions about their day to show that you care about their experiences beyond grades or achievements. For instance, ask,

"Who do you usually have lunch with?" or "What did you think of the group discussion today?"

6. Express Affection

Even as they grow older, teens still need love and reassurance. A daily hug or an "I love you" can go a long way in strengthening your bond.

7. Support Their Interests

Attend their events, such as sports games or performances, and express genuine appreciation for their efforts. Avoid critiquing their performance; instead, say, "I love watching you play."

8. Communicate Positively

Avoid focusing on their mistakes. Highlight their progress and successes, no matter how small. Positive reinforcement motivates them to improve and fosters cooperation.

9. Stay Connected Digitally

If direct communication feels challenging, texting can be an effective way to stay in touch. A quick message lets them know you're thinking of them without intruding.

10. Share Activities

Car Trips: Let them pick the playlist, even if it's not your taste. It opens a window into their personality. You may understand their thinking and perspectives.

Book Club: Read the same novel and discuss it together.

Workouts: Join them in activities they enjoy, like exercising.

Cooking: Collaborate on preparing meals or hosting dinners for their friends.

Volunteering: Work together on causes they care about, reinforcing shared values.

11. Respect Their Independence

Give them the freedom to make decisions, while calmly addressing your concerns. For example, if they want to attend a party, discuss safety and boundaries without being overly controlling.

12. Discuss Important Topics

Talk openly about relationships, dating, and safe sex. Creating a safe space for these conversations ensures they feel comfortable coming to you for guidance.

13. Rethink Discipline

Use mistakes as teaching moments. Instead of punishing, discuss their actions, the emotions behind them, and better ways to handle similar situations in the future.

14. Celebrate Their Uniqueness

Acknowledge their individuality and efforts, not just their achievements. Recognizing their perseverance during struggles boosts their self-esteem and reinforces your support.

15. Practice Unconditional Love

Parenting a teen requires patience and understanding. Just as a gardener nurtures a plant without blame, focus on identifying what your teen needs to thrive. Unconditional love is the foundation of a strong, trusting relationship.

Parenting during the teenage years may not always be smooth, but with empathy, open communication, and mutual respect, you can guide your teen toward adulthood while maintaining a strong, loving bond.

Balancing Emotions

Adolescence is a time of profound change, marked by emotional highs and lows. These mood shifts are a natural part of development as teens navigate physical, brain, social, and emotional changes. While such fluctuations are normal, extreme or prolonged moods that interfere with daily life may signal underlying mental health issues. Parents can play a pivotal role in helping their teens manage these changes by staying connected, offering support, and fostering independence.

Why Emotional Ups and Downs Happen?

1. Physical Factors

Adolescents undergo significant physical changes, including growth spurts and hormonal shifts, which can make them feel self-conscious or overwhelmed. Early or late physical development compared to peers can heighten these feelings.

Sleep also plays a crucial role in mood regulation. Pre-teens need 9–11 hours of sleep, while teens require 8–10 hours. Sleep deprivation can intensify mood swings. Nutrition and physical activity are equally vital; healthy eating and regular exercise often help stabilize emotions.

2. Brain Development

The adolescent brain undergoes continuous development, especially in the prefrontal cortex—the area responsible for managing emotions and decision-making. This region matures last, often into the early 20s, making it harder for teens to regulate intense emotions. Hormonal changes also introduce new and sometimes confusing romantic and sexual feelings.

3. Social and Emotional Factors

Teens face new responsibilities and challenges, such as navigating friendships, academic pressures, and family dynamics. They are also increasingly introspective, spending more time analyzing their thoughts and emotions. Stressful family situations can exacerbate mood fluctuations.

Helping Teens Experience More Ups Than Downs

1. Recognize Their Interests

Encourage your child to engage in activities they enjoy, whether it's sports, music, art, or creating digital content. These familiar activities provide a sense of security and a foundation for exploring new hobbies. Listen to their likes and dislikes to help identify activities that align with their passions.

2. Accept Emotional Fluctuations

Normalize emotional ups and downs by sharing your own experiences. Let your teen know it's okay to feel low sometimes and reassure them of your support during tough times. A simple acknowledgment like, "I can see you're having a hard day," can be comforting.

3. Stay Connected

Build trust and connection through everyday activities, like watching TV together or driving them somewhere. These casual moments often encourage teens to open up. Actively listen and stay attuned to what's happening in their life.

4. Give Them Space

Respect their need for independence and alone time to process emotions. Let them know you're available to talk when they're ready.

5. Collaborate on Solutions

Instead of solving problems for them, guide your teen to develop their own solutions. This fosters problem-solving skills and reinforces their ability to handle challenges independently.

6. Develop Coping Strategies Together

Help your teen identify healthy ways to manage emotional lows, such as listening to music, taking a walk, or watching a favourite movie.

7. Be a Role Model

Your child observes how you handle stress and emotions. Demonstrate healthy coping mechanisms and a positive attitude during challenging times to set a strong example.

Building Resilience and Trust

Helping teens navigate emotional ups and downs involves patience, empathy, and support. By understanding the reasons behind their moods, fostering open communication, and encouraging independence, you can equip your teen with the tools to manage their emotions effectively. Remember, the goal is not to eliminate challenges but to empower your child to handle them with confidence and resilience.

Mental Health Issues

Adolescence is a transformative and critical phase of life, characterized by physical, emotional, and social changes. These shifts, coupled with environmental and societal pressures, can make adolescents vulnerable to mental health challenges. Recognizing the signs of mental health issues early and fostering supportive environments can significantly impact an adolescent's overall well-being and future.

Adolescents may feel down or irritable for moments, hours, days, or even weeks. However, if a teen appears persistently sad, flat, or irritable for more than two weeks, or if their moods interfere with daily activities, it may indicate a serious mental health problem.

This stage is marked by rapid physical, emotional, and social changes. External factors like poverty, abuse, violence, or societal pressures can exacerbate mental health risks. Promoting resilience through social-emotional learning, access to mental healthcare, and supportive environments is essential for protecting adolescents from adversity.

Key Factors Affecting Adolescent Mental Health

Risk Factors

The more risks an adolescent is exposed to, the higher the likelihood of mental health issues. Key contributors include:

Adverse Experiences: Poverty, abuse, violence, and harsh parenting.

Peer Pressure and Identity Exploration: Pressure to conform and struggles with self-identity.

Media Influence and Gender Norms: Disparity between lived realities and perceived societal expectations.

Living Conditions: Adolescents in fragile settings or those experiencing stigma and discrimination face heightened risks.

Chronic Challenges: Chronic illnesses, disabilities, or being part of marginalized groups.

Common Mental Health Issues in Adolescence

Emotional Disorders: Anxiety and depression are the most prevalent, leading to school absences, social withdrawal, and, in severe cases, suicidal ideation.

Behavioral Disorders: Attention deficit hyperactivity disorder (ADHD) and conduct disorders, often emerging between ages 15-19, can disrupt education and lead to criminal behavior.

Eating Disorders: Conditions like anorexia nervosa and bulimia nervosa, characterized by abnormal eating behaviors and body image concerns, often surface during adolescence.

Psychosis: Late adolescence may bring symptoms like hallucinations and delusions, impairing daily life and increasing vulnerability to stigma.

Suicide: A leading cause of death among older adolescents, influenced by factors like substance abuse, childhood trauma, and access to means of suicide.

Recognizing and Addressing Teen Depression

Teen depression is a serious mental health condition marked by persistent sadness and a loss of interest in activities. Symptoms include:

Emotional Signs: Sadness, irritability, hopelessness, guilt, or self-criticism.

Behavioral Changes: Fatigue, social withdrawal, sleep disturbances, substance abuse, self-harm, or suicidal thoughts.

While some symptoms may stem from other causes, it's crucial to address persistent patterns by talking openly with your child and seeking professional help if necessary.

What Parents Can Do?

Promote Resilience and Healthy Habits

Encourage healthy sleep patterns, regular exercise, and balanced nutrition.

Help your child develop coping, problem-solving, and interpersonal skills.

Create a Supportive Environment

Foster a protective atmosphere at home, school, and within the community.

Address issues of stigma and discrimination.

Monitor and Communicate

Stay attentive to changes in behavior and mood.

Talk openly and empathetically, creating a safe space for your child to share feelings.

Be a Role Model

Demonstrate healthy coping strategies and resilience in your own life.

Seek Professional Help When Needed

If symptoms worsen or persist, consult a healthcare professional. Early intervention is key to managing mental health challenges effectively.

Hope and Patience

Addressing adolescent mental health requires time, patience, and faith. By staying connected and supportive, parents can guide their children through challenges, helping them build resilience and confidence. Remember, every challenge can be overcome with understanding, support, and professional guidance when needed.

Importance of Nutrition and Physical activity during Teenage

Importance of Nutrition during Teenage

Adolescence is a transformative phase characterized by rapid physical growth, sexual maturation, and significant hormonal changes. Nutrition is a critical factor during this period, shaping not only the immediate health of teenagers but also their future productivity, reproductive health, and resistance to diseases. Here's how parents can ensure their teenagers receive the essential nutrients needed for this vital stage of life.

Why Nutrition Matters During Teenage Years?

This stage of life brings a surge in physical growth, changes in body composition, and heightened energy needs. Poor dietary habits during adolescence can result in:

Stunted physical and mental development.

Increased complications in later life, especially for girls during pregnancy and childbirth.

A higher risk of chronic illnesses and reduced productivity in adulthood.

Making healthy lifestyle choices—including a balanced diet, regular physical activity, and adequate rest—can:

Strengthen bones and muscles.

Maintain a healthy body weight.

Enhance immunity.

Support emotional and mental well-being.

Key Nutritional Requirements for Teenagers

Carbohydrates

Function: Provide the primary source of energy.

Sources: Whole grains such as oats, brown rice, barley, and starchy vegetables.

Recommendation: At least half of daily grain consumption should consist of whole grains for sustained energy and fiber intake.

Proteins

Function: Support growth, repair tissues, and maintain healthy muscles, bones, and hormones.

Sources: Lean meats, eggs, legumes, nuts, seeds, and dairy products.

Fats

Function: Serve as a concentrated energy source and aid in hormonal regulation.

Healthy Sources: Avocados, nuts, seeds, and olive oil.

Limit: Saturated and trans fats found in processed and fast foods.

Vitamins and Minerals

Calcium and Vitamin D: Essential for bone growth and strength. Found in dairy, leafy greens, and fortified products.

Iron: Crucial for oxygen transport in the blood, especially important for menstruating girls. Found in lean meats, beans, and green vegetables.

Vitamin C: Boosts immunity and helps the body absorb iron. Found in citrus fruits, tomatoes, and bell peppers.

Fiber

Function: Promotes healthy digestion and prevents overeating.

Sources: Whole grains, fruits, vegetables, and legumes.

Vegetables

Teens should consume 2-4 cups daily, including a mix of dark green (spinach, broccoli), red/orange (carrots, pumpkin), and starchy (potatoes, corn) varieties.

Fruits

Opt for whole fruits over juices. Include options rich in vitamin C like oranges, berries, and kiwis to boost immunity and skin health.

Dairy Products

Ensure 2-3 servings of milk, yogurt, or cheese daily for calcium and vitamin D. Lactose-free and plant-based alternatives can be considered if necessary.

Snacks

Replace processed snacks with healthier choices like nuts, seeds, fresh fruits, and homemade options.

Hydration

Encourage water and natural drinks over sugary beverages to maintain energy levels and hydration.

Addressing Common Concerns in Adolescent Nutrition

Obesity and Overweight

Contributing Factors: Excessive screen time, consumption of sugary drinks, fast food, and lack of exercise.

Risks: Increased chances of heart disease, hormonal imbalances, and mental health issues.

Prevention: Promote balanced meals, encourage regular physical activity, and focus on portion control.

Iron-Deficiency Anemia

Causes: Low iron intake, heavy menstruation, or restrictive diets.

Symptoms: Fatigue, dizziness, pale skin, and weakness.

Prevention: Include iron-rich foods like spinach, fortified cereals, and lean meats. Pair these with vitamin C-rich foods for improved absorption.

Stunted Growth and Delayed Development

Poor nutrition during adolescence can lead to delayed physical growth, underdeveloped body structures, and slower sexual maturation.

Ensure a balanced diet and monitor for signs of deficiencies to support optimal growth.

Practical Tips for Parents

Teenagers are becoming more independent, often making their own food choices. They may skip meals, overindulge in unhealthy snacks, or follow fad diets. Here's how parents can help:

Prepare balanced meals at home and involve teens in meal planning.

Educate them on the importance of good nutrition and its long-term benefits.

Set a positive example by adopting healthy eating habits yourself.

Encourage open discussions about body image and avoid promoting unrealistic standards.

The Importance of Balanced Nutrition for Future Health

Teenagers require adequate nutrition to support their physical and mental growth. Nutritional deficiencies can lead to a lifetime of health challenges, including:

Delayed growth and development.

Reduced cognitive and emotional capacity.

Increased vulnerability to chronic illnesses.

Parents play a crucial role in guiding their teenagers toward healthier food and lifestyle choices. By prioritizing proper nutrition, physical activity, and emotional support, you can help your teenager thrive and set a strong foundation for adulthood.

Physical activity during teen years

Physical activity refers to any movement of the body, encompassing daily tasks, organized sports, and structured exercises. Regular exercise is a cornerstone of maintaining good health, especially for teenagers. Instilling healthy habits during childhood and adolescence lays the foundation for a lifetime of wellness, as behaviors adopted early are more likely to persist into adulthood. As people age, making significant lifestyle changes becomes more challenging, so starting early is essential.

The best way to encourage a healthy lifestyle is for the entire family to get involved. Physical activity should become a natural part of daily life, whether through sports, household chores, or dedicated exercises. The benefits of staying active include improved overall health, stronger bones and muscles, maintaining a healthy weight, enhanced mental clarity, better mood, and academic performance.

Additionally, it reduces the risk of chronic health conditions such as obesity, diabetes, and heart disease.

Teenagers should aim for at least 60 minutes of moderate to vigorous physical activity each day. Parents can foster healthy habits by limiting screen time and replacing sedentary behaviors with activities that involve movement. Even light to moderate activities, such as dancing or home workouts for 30 minutes daily, can be beneficial. Aerobic exercises, which increase heart and breathing rates, improve fitness levels and help prevent conditions like heart disease and type 2 diabetes. Examples of aerobic activities include running, gymnastics, hiking, and soccer. After physical exertion, teens should stay hydrated by drinking water or unsweetened fluids to prevent dehydration.

Consistent exercise also prevents weight gain, high blood pressure, unhealthy cholesterol levels, and other poor lifestyle choices that may lead to severe health issues like heart attacks or strokes later in life. However, it's essential to maintain a balance. Over-exercising can be harmful, leading to weight loss below healthy levels or interfering with daily responsibilities such as school. If this happens, it's crucial to guide your teen toward a healthier balance and ensure they prioritize overall well-being over physical appearance.

Physical activity not only strengthens the body but also sharpens the mind. It builds confidence and instils a zest for life, acting as a catalyst for growth and positivity. However, exercise alone isn't enough. Like balanced nutrition, adequate sleep is equally vital for a healthy lifestyle. Sleep directly affects mood, decision-making abilities, and even weight management. Teens should aim for 8-9 hours of sleep each night.

To promote healthy sleep patterns:

Establish a consistent bedtime and wake-up routine.

Encourage regular physical activity during the day.

Avoid heavy meals close to bedtime.

Limit screen time an hour before sleep.

A healthy lifestyle that includes regular exercise, proper nutrition, and sufficient rest sets the stage for a brighter, more energetic future. Teens who embrace these habits are more likely to grow into confident, calm, and driven individuals. In contrast, neglecting these aspects can lead to aggression, apathy, and a lack of enthusiasm for life.

Parents play a pivotal role in this journey. Children learn best by example, so before encouraging your child to adopt a healthier lifestyle, make the changes yourself. By doing so, you'll inspire your entire family to embrace a path of health and vitality together.

Importance of Spiritualism in Teenage

Teenage years are a pivotal stage in life, marked by identity exploration and decision-making that can shape the future. Studies highlight that teenagers with a clear sense of meaning and purpose experience numerous benefits, such as resilience, healthy self-esteem, academic engagement, and overall well-being. Those who understand their life's purpose tend to report greater happiness and reduced stress, alongside a more positive self-image. Additionally, a sense of meaning enhances academic performance by fostering better adjustments to school life, goal-oriented learning, and satisfaction with educational experiences. It motivates teenagers to connect their studies to real-life applications, fostering creativity and critical thinking—qualities that contribute to the development of well-rounded individuals.

Adolescence is an ideal time to encourage this search for meaning. When teenagers feel a lack of purpose, they may experience boredom, which can lead to disengagement from learning and impulsive behavior. Spirituality, or the practice of finding deeper meaning and purpose in life, can play a vital role here. It equips teens with the emotional resilience needed to navigate this transitional phase and strengthens their ability to build meaningful relationships while maintaining open communication with their parents.

As teenagers grow, their curiosity evolves into creativity and a desire for adventure, often accompanied by risk-taking tendencies. While this exploration is natural, it can lead to impulsive actions or defiance of societal norms. Teens are in the process of discovering their identity, a journey that involves trial and error. They require support and guidance to understand the difference between right and wrong. Spirituality can provide this guidance, helping them make better decisions, develop emotional balance, and foster self-awareness.

The competitive pressures of today's world further complicate adolescence. Many teenagers face immense stress to outperform their peers, leading to negative emotions such as jealousy and the temptation to take unethical shortcuts. Technological distractions also contribute to a fast-paced lifestyle that can leave teens restless and easily bored. Without proper guidance, they may turn to harmful behaviors like substance abuse or irresponsible actions in search of happiness.

Spirituality can act as a stabilizing force, offering teens a sense of belonging, improved self-worth, and the tools to build positive relationships. It fosters hope during difficult times, reduces stress and anxiety, and encourages healthier lifestyle choices. **Teens who practice spirituality often report stronger connections with their families, better emotional regulation, and a greater sense of purpose in life.**

Incorporating spiritual practices into family life can help teenagers build a strong foundation. This might include teaching them about family traditions, engaging in yoga and mindfulness exercises, spending time in nature, or exploring creative outlets like writing, art, and music. Encouraging stillness and quiet reflection, even for a few minutes daily, can enhance focus and patience. Activities that involve physical movement, such as dancing, swimming, or hiking, can also foster a sense of connection with the body and nature. Acts of service, such as helping others, develop empathy and compassion while reinforcing the interconnectedness of life.

Meditation, whether through breathing exercises, silent contemplation, or chanting, is another powerful tool to guide teens toward inner peace and clarity. **Spirituality does not require religious affiliation; it is an individual journey of self-discovery. It helps teenagers understand their values, strengths, and the broader purpose of their lives. This self-awareness enables them to make decisions that align with long-term goals and cultivate meaningful relationships.**

True spirituality is a personal journey that does not require public displays or validation. It is about fostering inner growth and allowing one's actions and successes to speak for themselves. A healthy spiritual practice can transform the way teens navigate challenges, helping them develop resilience, clarity, and a sense of fulfillment.

By embracing spirituality as a family, parents can model behaviors that inspire teenagers to follow suit. As children often learn by observing their parents, creating a spiritually enriched environment can positively influence their journey. Begin this process for your family's well-being, ensuring a supportive and nurturing atmosphere that promotes growth, understanding, and happiness.

Parenting your Teenager

Things to Avoid during Parenting a Teenager

The transition from childhood to teenage years seems to happen in the blink of an eye. While you, as a parent, may feel largely the same, your child has grown and changed significantly. Parenting strategies that were effective when your child was 5 years old may no longer work now that they are 15. Unfortunately, sticking to outdated parenting methods can lead to challenges and misunderstandings.

Research highlights that teenagers tend to thrive when they share open and honest communication with their parents. Teens who report strong communication with their mother or father are less likely to engage in risky behaviors. Furthermore, studies have confirmed that parents are the most significant influence on their teen's decisions regarding family values, expectations, and sensitive topics like drugs and sex. To foster a positive relationship with your teenager and support their development, it's essential to recognize and avoid common parenting mistakes.

Staying in Tune with Your Teen's World

As parents, it's crucial to stay informed and adapt just as we regularly update our devices or apps. The more we understand, the better equipped we'll be to guide and support our teenagers. If we're unaware of the pressures and attractions that shape their world, it becomes difficult to respond appropriately or offer effective guidance. Take the time to read and learn about the physical, emotional, and social changes teenagers experience, such as acne and braces, mood swings, peer pressure, growing curiosity about relationships and sex, increased risk-taking tendencies, temptations like substance use (alcohol, tobacco, or drugs), fashion trends, entertainment choices, and the impact of social media. Staying updated will help bridge the gap between you and your teen, enabling you to navigate their challenges with empathy and understanding.

Preparing Your Teen for the Teenage Years

In previous generations, many of us stumbled through our teenage years without much guidance or preparation for the changes we faced. However, that approach is no longer sufficient. Today's teens must navigate an overwhelming influx of social media, digital content, and societal pressures. It's essential to prepare them for the challenges ahead, but this doesn't mean lecturing or being overly formal.

Instead, aim for casual, meaningful conversations. Spend quality time together, such as watching movies, and use those moments to discuss relevant topics afterward. Building this connection helps you understand what's going on in your teen's mind and heart.

During puberty, both boys and girls experience significant physical changes. It's vital to discuss these openly to prevent misunderstandings and body shaming. In a world dominated by social media, advertisements, and TV commercials that often promote unrealistic standards, your role is to teach your teen how to identify and avoid harmful influences. Address these issues early and constructively, empowering them to embrace self-confidence and a healthy self-image.

Listening More Than Talking- Lecturing your teen might seem like a natural response, but it's often counterproductive. Teens typically don't respond well to long lectures and may even shut down. Instead, they want to be heard. Even if you disagree with them, it's crucial they feel understood and know that their feelings are valid. Listening more than speaking can help foster a stronger relationship with your teen.

Of course, they still need your guidance, but it's important to approach it wisely. Keep your words short, clear, and to the point. Avoid repeating yourself or sounding monotonous. Share real-life examples that they can relate to, and try to involve them in problem-solving by asking questions that prompt them to think critically. Rather than asking "why," which can feel confrontational, try "how" or "what" questions to encourage a more open dialogue.

In addition to addressing problems, use these moments to talk about broader topics that are important for their development, such as relationships, consent, safe touch, and personal boundaries. Regularly carve out time to have open discussions about these topics. If you feel uncomfortable, use factual explanations to provide clarity and understanding. When your teen has clear guidance on what's right and wrong, they're less likely to make poor choices.

It's natural to feel upset when your teen lies to you, but the way you respond can either worsen the situation or lead to better understanding. For instance, if you learn that your child skipped class and lied about it, your first instinct may be to punish them. However, punishment might only encourage them to find better ways to lie in the future. Instead, try to approach the situation with empathy. Ask them what happened, and understand their reasoning behind the action. Perhaps they skipped class because they were unprepared for an exam or feared a confrontation.

By listening first and addressing the situation calmly, you show your teen that you value their perspective. Studies suggest that when parents understand their child's point of view before asserting their own, it fosters increased self-esteem and better emotional regulation in children. This approach not only helps resolve conflicts but also builds trust and respect.

Having low expectations from your teen- There's a saying, **"Treat a person as they are, and they will remain as they are. Treat a person as they can and should be, and they will become what they can and should be."** This principle applies directly to parenting. Set high goals and expectations for your teen, and provide them with the support and guidance needed to reach them. When you believe in their potential and encourage them to aim high, it helps them believe in themselves too.

Don't judge their future by their present behavior. Teenagers are still growing and evolving, and their capabilities are far from fixed. Your teen may not show signs of brilliance today, but with the right guidance and encouragement, they can excel in ways you may not expect. It's important to help them build resilience and prepare for all situations, whether positive or negative.

Parenting isn't about simply giving your child everything they want. It's about teaching them the skills and mindset to achieve their goals and aspirations the right way. Guide them to be capable, responsible, and independent individuals who are ready to face the challenges of the future.

The Need for Privacy in Parenting

As your teen grows, they will naturally begin to seek more privacy. You might hear them say things like, "I want my space" or "I'm talking to my friend on the phone, I need privacy." This desire for privacy is completely normal and can be a sign of their growing independence. Allowing your teen some personal space shows that you trust them and respect their need for boundaries. However, it's important to find a balance between privacy and supervision.

While giving your teen space is necessary, setting clear ground rules can help ensure they are safe and responsible. For example, consider keeping the computer or any device with internet access in a shared family area. This allows you to be aware of their online activity while still respecting their need for privacy. You can also use parental control software to monitor their online time and activity, ensuring they are using the internet safely.

Encourage your teen to bring their friends home, and make it a point to know where they are spending time outside. Being involved in their social life doesn't mean invading their privacy, but rather showing interest in their well-being and providing guidance when needed. Additionally, consider becoming their "silent friend" on social media platforms like Facebook. By following their online activities discreetly, you can stay informed about who they are interacting with and ensure they are navigating the digital world responsibly.

Finding the right balance between privacy and supervision is key to maintaining a trusting and open relationship with your teen.

Good grades don't always mean a well-adjusted teen – Many parents mistakenly assume that a high academic performance guarantees their teen is thriving and safe. However, countless bright students with excellent grades face challenges such as drug use, bullying, negative peer influence, and low self-esteem. It's crucial to stay alert to any signs of behavioral issues and address them promptly.

Dismissing their problems – It's easy to overlook your teen's concerns when you're dealing with more significant issues yourself. However, if you want to build trust and encourage open communication, it's essential to understand their perspective. What might seem minor or trivial to you can feel like a major crisis to your teen. Statements like "This won't matter in the future," "You're overreacting," or "It's not worth getting upset about" can make them feel dismissed and misunderstood. Instead of downplaying their feelings, focus on helping them find solutions. This approach not only strengthens their problem-solving abilities but also shows them you genuinely care about their experiences, no matter how small they may seem.

Resisting the urge to solve their problems – Watching your teen face challenges can be tough, but stepping in to fix things for them does more harm than good. To prepare them for adulthood, they need to develop the skills to handle problems independently. While empathy allows you to understand their feelings, over-identifying with their struggles—feeling them as if they were your own—can unintentionally rob them of valuable growth experiences. Sharing in their joys and hardships is natural, but taking on their problems as your own prevents them from forming their own perspectives, learning resilience, and building problem-solving skills. It's important to support them without taking ownership of their challenges.

Avoiding dismissiveness toward their ideas – Teens often come up with grand ideas that may seem unrealistic. Dismissing these ideas outright can discourage them and make them reluctant to share their thoughts in the future. Instead, approach their ideas with curiosity. You don't have to agree or praise the idea, but asking questions like "What excites you about this?" or "How do you plan to make it work?" shows genuine interest and support. This approach not only strengthens your connection but also encourages them to think critically, helping them evaluate the feasibility of their ideas on their own.

Being disrespectful- While parents often feel disrespected by their teens, the reverse can also be true. If your teen feels disrespected by you, they are unlikely to open up or communicate freely. Respect is a two-way street—parents cannot expect to receive respect without giving it in return. Teens learn respect best when their parents model it for them.

It's natural to feel hurt if your teen seems to take you for granted, rejects you, or acts out. But this behavior isn't personal; it's a normal part of growing up. Teens are often preoccupied, testing boundaries, or struggling to regulate their emotions. You're their safe space, and they know your love is unconditional. That's why they may direct their frustrations at you.

Instead of taking it personally, remember that their behavior reflects their struggles, not their feelings about you. If your teen says or does something hurtful, give yourself time to process before addressing it. A calm, productive conversation later is more effective than reacting in the heat of the moment.

Think of it like a mother breastfeeding her baby—the baby might kick or squirm, but the mother doesn't take it personally or stop feeding. Similarly, when your teen misbehaves, recognize that they're still learning and growing. Give them space, patience, and understanding. As they mature, they'll return to you for guidance and support. Parenting requires patience, emotional control, and consistency, as the behavior you model will shape your child's future actions and attitudes.

Avoid expecting your teen to fit a mold – Every teen is unique, and each requires a different approach to parenting. Some may respond well to simple explanations, others might need motivation or detailed guidance, while a few may only grasp lessons through real-life examples. There are also teens who may not understand even after several attempts, requiring even more patience and perseverance.

As a parent, it's important not to compare your children or expect them to behave or learn in the same way. Instead, focus on teaching them the right behaviors and values, tailoring your approach to their individual needs. With patience and consistent effort, you can guide them effectively, helping them grow into their best selves.

Avoid Sending Mixed Messages as Parents- Consistency is key in parenting, and it's crucial for both parents to be aligned in their approach. If one parent undermines the other by interfering or shielding the child, it can disrupt the entire parenting process. Parents need to function as a team, working together toward the same goals. Depending on the situation, you may need to adjust your parenting style—whether it's being strict, lenient, or supportive. But ultimately, both parents must collaborate to provide a unified front and act in the best interest of their child.

Involve Teens in Household Decisions- Including your teen in family decisions is an excellent way to build their sense of responsibility and independence. When you invite them to share their opinions, they feel valued and gain valuable skills needed for adulthood. It's a simple yet impactful way to teach them about decision-making and accountability.

Avoid Forcing Conversations Into Your Timetable- Teens often open up spontaneously, not when it's most convenient for you. You can't schedule meaningful conversations like a meeting. Your teen may choose to share their thoughts when you're stressed or busy with other tasks. In those moments, it's important to set aside your own priorities and listen. If you dismiss them, they might hesitate to open up again.

Seize these opportunities for connection, as the warmest and most rewarding conversations happen when your teen feels ready to talk and you make time for them. Prioritize connection over correction, and embrace this phase of parenting despite its challenges.

Bridge the Gap During Teenage Years.The teenage years can create a natural distance between you and your child. It's essential for one of you to make the effort to close that gap. If left unaddressed, it may linger into adulthood. Use this time to rediscover your bond with your teen—a relationship that, with patience and understanding, can grow into a lifelong connection.

Stopping Influence of Wrong People on my Teenager

Watching your child grow from a dependent, affectionate kid into an independent teen can be bittersweet. As they begin spending more time with friends and less with family, parents often worry about the influence of their peer group. Negative influences can manifest in behaviors like skipping classes, engaging in unlawful activities, lying, poor academic performance, loss of interest in hobbies, or even adopting rude or violent behavior. Protecting your teen from bad influences requires a thoughtful, balanced approach. Here are some strategies:

1. Avoid Criticism

Criticizing your teen's friends can backfire, as teens are naturally defensive about their choices. If you openly disapprove of a friend, your teen may feel compelled to defend them and may dismiss your concerns entirely. Instead, take a more neutral approach when discussing their friends.

2. Encourage Expanding Their Friend Circle

Encourage your teen to meet new people and expand their friend group without outright discouraging their current friendships. Casually suggest activities or opportunities where they might interact with others who share positive traits you value. This subtle approach allows them to form healthier friendships without feeling forced.

3. Share Observations Without Judgment

Instead of criticizing, calmly share observations about behaviors you find concerning. For example, you might say, "I noticed [friend's name] often skips school. What do you think about that?" This approach helps your teen recognize problematic behavior on their own and encourages critical thinking.

4. Set Boundaries

If you're concerned about a friend's influence, establish clear boundaries. For instance, encourage them to spend time with their friends at your home, where you can observe the dynamic. Set reasonable curfews and check in about their plans without being overly intrusive.

5. Communicate Openly

If your concerns persist, have an honest conversation with your teen. Share your fears and reservations calmly, focusing on your teen's feelings and perspectives rather than solely on the friend. Listen actively and try to understand their point of view, fostering a more open and productive dialogue.

6. Engage with the Friend's Parents

If you know the friend's parents, consider discussing your concerns with them. They may share similar observations or be unaware of their child's behavior. Working together can help both families address the situation effectively.

7. Consult Your Teen's Teachers

Teachers often have valuable insights into your teen's social dynamics and behavior at school. Reach out to them to see if they've noticed anything concerning. Their observations can help you better understand the situation and guide your next steps.

8. Seek Professional Support if Needed

If the situation becomes overwhelming or doesn't improve, consider consulting a counsellor. A professional can help your teen navigate their emotions, develop better decision-making skills, and address any underlying issues contributing to their choices.

Bridging the Gap

Parenting a teenager comes with unique challenges, but it also offers opportunities to strengthen your bond. Teens are navigating complex social and emotional changes, and your support can make a significant difference. By staying patient, empathetic, and proactive, you can help your teen make healthier choices and maintain a positive relationship that lasts a lifetime.

Influence of Media on Teenagers

Media has an undeniable ability to shape the thoughts and beliefs of teenagers, who are often impressionable and curious. With technological advancements, media has become a significant part of daily life. However, its continuous exposure impacts teens' physical, psychological, and social development, both positively and negatively.

Positive Impacts of Media on Teens

A Platform for Entertainment and Self-Expression

Social media provides a space for teens to connect with like-minded individuals worldwide, fostering confidence and self-esteem. It also serves as a creative outlet for self-expression.

Source of Inspiration

Inspirational content such as documentaries, movies, and real-life success stories can motivate teens to set and achieve goals.

Development of Social Skills

Social media offers introverted teens a low-pressure environment to interact, helping them build social skills essential for effective communication.

Awareness of Social and Political Issues

Media can spark interest in current events, encouraging teens to engage with topics like poverty, global warming, and social justice. This exposure can shape their personality and broaden their worldview.

Health Awareness

Media platforms disseminate valuable information on health and well-being. Teens who engage with such content are more likely to understand issues like depression, obesity, and their solutions, encouraging informed lifestyle choices.

Aids in Identity Formation

Quality media content can influence teens' values and identity. For instance, movies promoting gender equality can inspire teens to adopt these principles in their lives.

Negative Impacts of Media on Teens

Health and Development Issues

Excessive screen time is linked to poor academic performance, sleep deprivation, reduced physical activity, and limited face-to-face interactions. These factors contribute to obesity and hinder overall development.

Unrealistic Body Image

Media often promotes unattainable beauty standards, negatively impacting teens' self-esteem and body image.

Promotion of Harmful Behaviors

Media can glamorize harmful habits like smoking, drinking, or reckless driving, influencing teens to mimic such behaviors to appear "cool."

Spreading Incorrect Beliefs

Biased information and fake news shared on social platforms can instill stereotypes and misconceptions, shaping teens' attitudes and behaviors negatively.

Mental Health Concerns

Exposure to cyberbullying, peer pressure, and idealized portrayals of others' lives can lead to depression, anxiety, isolation, and even suicidal thoughts.

Encouragement of Violent Behavior

Studies show a correlation between exposure to violent TV shows or video games and increased aggression in teens, potentially altering their behavior.

Media Addiction

Overuse of social media or gaming platforms can lead to addiction-like behaviors. Teens may become fixated on likes, shares, and validation from peers, creating a cycle of dependency and lowering their focus on real-life responsibilities.

Parental Guidance is Key To protect teens from the negative impacts of media:

Monitor the quality and quantity of content they consume.

Encourage open discussions about media messages and their implications.

Set boundaries for screen time and ensure a balance between online and offline activities.

Teach critical thinking skills to help them differentiate between trustworthy and misleading information.

Taking proactive steps can help your teen harness the positive aspects of media while minimizing its potential downsides. After all, prevention is always better than facing challenges later. As parenting is all about patience and alertness.

Motivating and Inspiring your Teenager to find Passion in life

As a parent, it's natural to wonder about the kind of adults your children will become, what professions they'll choose, and what their futures will look like. Teenagers face many distractions, especially due to hormonal and emotional imbalances, and their journey toward discovering their passions can be complex. Some teens are born with a clear passion, while others may need a little encouragement to find theirs. Every child is different. **According to a survey, only 20% of individuals aged 12 to 22 have a lasting, specific passion, while the rest may have general interests or hobbies but struggle to commit to a clear direction.**

Passion is what drives us to dedicate time and energy to something we love, something that excites and fulfills us. It's what makes us feel alive, creating meaning in our lives. Passion gives us guidance, direction, and structure. For teenagers, however, the biggest obstacle is often a lack of experience—they simply haven't had the chance to explore many areas of life. As a parent, you can help them explore different activities and experiences, which will build their confidence and help them eventually discover their passion.

It's important to recognize that finding a life purpose and choosing a career are two separate journeys. Teens may engage in hobbies that don't seem directly related to future careers, but that's okay. Not every passion leads to a job, but each one can contribute to personal growth. For example, a passion might help develop valuable soft skills like creativity, teamwork, or resilience, which are essential in any career. Other times, a passion might evolve into a side project or hobby that provides a sense of accomplishment and identity beyond work. The key is to encourage exploration and balance, helping your teen find satisfaction in both their professional and personal lives.

Ways to Help Your Teen Discover Their Passion

Understand Their Interests

Start by engaging in open conversations with your teen. Ask questions like, "What brings me joy?" "What activity makes me lose track of time?" "Who do I look up to?" or "What's the highlight of my day at school?" These questions encourage self-reflection and help your teen discover what excites them. Encourage introspection by identifying moments when they feel truly engaged or in a "flow state"—times when they're absorbed in an activity and forget about everything else.

Explore the World Together

The world is changing rapidly, with new developments and trends emerging all the time. Explore different advancements and activities together to see what resonates with your teen's interests and passions.

Provide Resources and Opportunities

Once you understand your teen's interests, provide the necessary resources and opportunities for them to explore those passions further. Encourage them to attend events or join communities where they can meet like-minded individuals.

Seek Mentors

A mentor can play a significant role in helping your teen explore their passion. Introduce them to professionals or people who are passionate about their work. Arrange interviews or shadowing opportunities so your teen can learn about different careers and gain insight into what those roles entail.

Create a Supportive Environment

At home, show genuine interest in your teen's activities. Discuss their progress, challenges, and achievements. Offer encouragement when they face difficulties, and celebrate milestones together.

Help Set Realistic Goals

Help your teen set realistic, achievable goals by breaking down larger objectives into smaller, manageable steps. This approach fosters a sense of accomplishment and keeps them motivated. Encourage them to stay organized and track their progress with timelines or schedules.

Encourage a Vision for the Future

Vision boards can be a powerful tool for manifesting goals. Encourage your teen to create a vision board that represents their aspirations, keeping it visible to inspire them daily.

Challenge Them

Encourage your teen to step out of their comfort zone by trying new activities and exploring different fields. Participate in extracurricular activities, volunteer opportunities, and cultural events to help them discover new passions. Teach them to view challenges as opportunities for growth and to embrace a growth mindset.

Handling Teens with Low Passion

Parenting a teen with low passion can be frustrating, but patience and support are key. Push, nudge, and encourage them to take responsibility for their commitments, while maintaining faith that they will eventually discover their purpose.

The Rocking Chair Test

This exercise involves picturing yourself as an older person looking back at your life. Ask yourself how the decisions you make today will affect your future. Would you regret not pursuing a passion? This exercise can provide clarity and motivation for making meaningful choices today.

As a parent, you play a crucial role in guiding your teen through this transformative stage. By encouraging them to explore their passions, providing resources, and supporting their journey, you help them build the foundation for a fulfilling future. Every teen's path is unique, and while it may take time, with your encouragement and guidance, they will eventually find their purpose. Remember, the journey of self-discovery is not always linear, and each experience can bring them closer to understanding what truly ignites their passion.

Parenting is not about giving everything they need, but make them capable to which whatever they want. Make them capable to face hardships of life and stay happy and satisfied. Make them capable to face hardships of life to become best version of themselves. Not only them even you, when we try to become best version of ourselves, we get best opportunities and best everything.

Teaching Values and Ethics to my Teenager

Moral values play a crucial role in shaping a child's personality, especially during their teenage years. These values help them navigate the complexities of life and make the right decisions even when faced with difficult situations. Teaching children the difference between right and wrong provides them with a moral compass, allowing them to stay on track and resist negative influences as they grow. When children understand and embrace good values, they become more accountable, responsible, and honest individuals. These values not only influence their character but also boost their self-confidence, helping them remain positive even in challenging circumstances.

In previous part that is parenting early childhood, I have shared a lot of information of values and ethics, but now in this age the parenting style need to be changed, because- In today's culture, where unethical behavior is often glamorized, teens are bombarded with mixed messages. Peer pressure, media, and even the actions of adults can lead them to question the importance of integrity. The key is to provide clear guidance on why good values matter, not just through vague advice but by helping them understand the reasons behind ethical behavior. Teenagers face tough ethical dilemmas every day, from cheating to lying, from peer pressure to experimentation with substances. It's essential to equip them with the tools to make responsible choices.

Here are ways to help guide teens in developing and maintaining moral values:

Focus on Values: Counteract negative cultural messages by consistently reinforcing the importance of good values. Share positive ethical stories from the media or books to initiate conversations about right and wrong.

Label Them Good: Help teens define themselves as good people who are still learning. Avoid labelling them with negative terms like "cheater" or "liar." When they make mistakes, remind them that it's just a detour and guide them back to the right path.

Help Them Find Their Contribution: Encourage teens to use their strengths and interests to make a positive impact on their community. This helps them discover purpose and solidify their moral identity.

Be a Good Role Model: Children learn by imitation. If you want them to be honest, generous, or responsible, model those behaviors yourself.

Watch for Teaching Moments: Everyday situations offer valuable opportunities to discuss values. Whether it's a news story about courage or a real-life example of disrespect, use these moments to teach valuable lessons.

Offer a Broader Perspective: Encourage your teen to think beyond themselves and consider the impact of their choices on others, the community, and society as a whole. Help them understand that ethical decisions often benefit the greater good.

Have Frequent Conversations About Values: Make values a regular topic of discussion in your household, not just when something goes wrong. This will help your teen internalize their importance.

Serve Others Together: Volunteering and helping others is a powerful way to instill values in your child. Take opportunities to serve together, demonstrating how actions speak louder than words.

Create Open Communication: Ask open-ended questions that prompt your teen to think about ethical dilemmas they might face. Avoid expressing judgment, as this may make them defensive. Use "I" statements to share your own perspective.

Help Them Stay the Course During Hard Times: Encourage resilience. Life is full of challenges, and it's essential to teach your teen not to quit when things get tough. Reinforce the value of perseverance and confidence.

Praise Them When They Uphold Their Values: Positive reinforcement is key. When your teen demonstrates honesty, responsibility, or other values, praise them for making the right choice, even if it was difficult.

Share Your Own Stories: By sharing your personal experiences—both the challenges and the rewards of making ethical decisions—you help your teen understand the real-world consequences of their actions.

Ask Thought-Provoking Questions: Instead of dictating what values your teen should hold, ask them questions that encourage reflection and dialogue. These questions help them think critically about their beliefs and make informed choices.

Be Transparent About Your Own Struggles: Show your teen that making the right choice is not always easy. Share your own struggles with ethical decisions and explain how you navigate them. This helps them understand that everyone makes mistakes and that making the right choice is a process.

By actively engaging in these practices, you can help your teen develop strong moral values that will guide them through life's challenges. By being a role model, having open conversations, and providing opportunities for growth, you empower your teen to make ethical decisions and contribute positively to society.

Now after this age and following parenting techniques your mini adults is ready to be a youth. The role of parents won't stop here, but style is changed. So happy parenting!!!

PART 4

PARENTING YOUNGSTER

'Being a parent of a youth'

We have completed more than 60% of the parenting journey and are approaching its final phase. However, this does not mean that the journey or the relationship will come to an end, as the parenting style evolves. At this stage, your child is no longer just a kid, but a young adult. They will begin to lead their own life independently. Until now, you have protected and supported them in every aspect, but now your child has reached a point where they are not only physically equal to you but also share responsibilities.

At this point, they become more of a friend, supporter, strength, and source of mutual encouragement. They must take on responsibilities and begin to fulfill their lifelong obligations. The balance between you and your child is now equal, with both of you sharing everything equally.

It is important to understand that many parents mistakenly believe that when their children are nearing the end of their education or are about to enter the workforce, the role of a parent diminishes. They often assume that if their children are happy, they are happy, and thus end this precious journey. This mindset, however, overlooks the continued significance of the parent-child relationship.

Take a moment to reflect: do you still share the same strong bond with your parents as you did during your childhood? There have been many changes over time. You may find that you hardly spend time with them now, as your focus has shifted to your own success and family. However, it's important to remember that everything you have today—whether it's your career, wealth, or even your family— is a result of your parents' sacrifices and care. The saying is true: the value of a person can only truly be understood when you are in their position. Ask yourself; don't you miss the days when you could rest peacefully in your mother's lap, free from worries and stress, or the feeling of safety under your father's roof? But now, you may no longer have those comforts. Even your parents, who need you, may long for those days.

While you may be in a better position than others, let us not forget the unfortunate reality of some children who have rejected their parents, sending them to old age homes or abandoning them without reason. Always remember, what we do comes back to us—it's a cycle. When your parents were old, you were young and may have rejected their responsibilities. But soon, you will grow older, and your children will be in the same position. Let us hope and pray that the cycle remains one of respect, love, and responsibility, rather than repetition of past mistakes.

Soon, you will grow older, just as your child is young, energetic, and responsible enough to provide you with a fulfilling retirement and a happy life. I wish and pray that this is the reality of your relationship with your child. Imagine what your retirement stage would look like. While you may think of job retirement, I am referring to **life retirement**. This is the time when you will finally relax, enjoy every moment, and fulfill the dreams and passions you couldn't pursue earlier. You'll spend quality time with your life partner, whom you may have had to compromise time with for the sake of your children. You'll reconnect with family and friends, who you couldn't afford to, spend time with because of your responsibilities toward your kids. You'll feel proud and elated at the milestones your child achieves. Most importantly, your relationship with your child will be as strong and harmonious as it was before—working together as a team to navigate life's challenges and successes. As a happy, ideal family with no differences, this is the kind of retirement life that you should aspire to. After all the struggles and sacrifices life has presented, don't you deserve such a retirement?

Parents, be honest with yourselves. Don't repeat the mistakes your own parents made. Both you and your parents have suffered, so learn from that, grow, and think practically. Everyone needs support in life, and you probably understand this better than anyone. If you had the full support of your parents, wouldn't you have reached the peak of your success without making so many mistakes? Normally, people learn from their own mistakes, but successful individuals learn from others' mistakes. If you had the experience, support, and wisdom of your parents throughout your life, you would have saved time, energy, and even money. Staying with family fosters a sense of security, responsibility, and wisdom.

So,as I am a daughter of a businessman, according to me, Parenting is indeed an investment, and the returns you receive come in the form of a fulfilling and peaceful retirement life. A true investor understands that the value of their investment multiplies over time, yielding profits in the long run. Similarly, the effort, love, and care you invest in raising your children will eventually reward you with their support, companionship, and gratitude as they grow older. So, parents, the question is: are you a true investor in your child's life? If the answer is yes, then it's crucial to consider how to make this investment successful. To ensure a fruitful return, here are a few key principles:

Forming a strong bond- emotions are foundation of any relationship. Being emotionally connected with your youth is very important. The bond is already present from beginning of parenthood journey now you have to change little bit, almost similar to teenage but no need of any curtains. It showed be totally open. There should be no difference, just like a friend of your age. As you bond with your friend it should be similar and even more closer like soul and body, no difference. In previous section I have told how to bond with them, they should be sharing everything to you almost but from your side it was just 50-60% now make it 100%. Discuss about you everything, household decisions, finance, work problems, family issues, health conditions even your personal problem with your life partner which you can't share with anyone. By this the bond would get deeper and deeper.

Your bond should be so deep that no relation, problem should be a crack between you. You may always think I wish I have someone with whom I can share anything even those things that can't be said to anyone can be now said to your youth. Don't forget your child is a part of you not a different person. Think your child as your heart, you keep all your things in your heart right and can't live without it. Similarly for your child.

Giving all your life experiences and knowledge- now this is very important, till now you had given what was necessary in that age. But now you are preparing them for action. So no compromise. Now you should share all good and bad experiences you had. Your failure, your success, mistakes etc. Don't hide anything from them. The more transparent you be, the same behaviour would be reflected by your youth. Share stories and journey of your younger days. Share all the knowledge you learnt till now, whether it is managing finance, household work, communication skills, dealing with stress in life, dressing and grooming skills, even about romance.

Sharing responsibilities- now your child is a youth. Now he/she would enter the world and face challenges of life. So, it's your duty to prepare them for the future. When your child gets into his/her professional course, you should begin the training. By the time they finish and enter the world for earning they should be capable enough to face hardships of life and gain success. Now question is how to give them training. First start with small challenges slowly increase the intensity. By this there capacity of facing more than two challenges would be increased. First challenge them to pursue their professional course not only for certification but gain complete knowledge, even encourage them to think beyond the box of their field. Secondly, ask them develop special skills that are required in present world. Third, give them full responsibilities of household for example bringing all the groceries by themselves, by this they would learn value of food and money, learn to manage finance, and also bargaining skills with communication. Start giving responsibilities slowly year by year like in first year of their professional course ask them to focus only on professional course with extra skills related to that, then start giving responsibilities slowly slowly by seeing their capacity. They may do some mistakes while handling, you have to take care patiently, as they are learning. According to me "parenting during this age, is about surprises, so that they don't get surprised when life gives it". Once you think that they are capable of handling all household work that is management of complete budget, start giving challenges, like give all the amount and say them to manage finance themselves for a year for the whole house. Let them take all the decisions about expenses, savings everything on their own. Initially they may do some mistakes just guide them but don't jump to solve, let them solve whatever it may be. Majority of people don't know how to balance these expenses and savings, it takes years to learn. By this challenge your child won't need to appoint his/her life, as they are all ready with perfection under your guidance. Let them continue this as their daily routine with coming new challenges.

Preparing them for future- in previous point I said of normal responsibilities. When you have checked that your child is capable of handling all responsibilities related to household and their profession. We will start giving next level of training that is somewhat similar to what our life gives. You may think what I am saying, just like preparatory before finals or pre match before finals. You can begin by giving deadline for their daily work (responsibilities given), this increases there capacity to tolerate pressure and stress. Then ask them to handle two or more works simultaneously, so in future they can sort all these problems at a time. Then ask them to manage all the expenses in half of the budget. By this they will learn about maintaining expenses when they have financial problems. Then to show them reality that is how difficult it is to make life in such a fast world. Take them to your work place, expose them to different types of people to learn how to differentiate between good and bad people and how to deal with them, by this chances of getting cheated by someone would be reduced. And their will boost in their confidence and alertness towards outside world when they step out. Show them how you work, what are your dreams and aspirations that you couldn't fulfil, this would encourage and motivate them and also give a reality check that all dreams won't come true, and not necessary that we will always win. This will make them set real goals and work with costiveness and balance their emotions during failure.

Teaching importance of family and relationships- teaching and handling of inside world is equally important as of facing outside world. It's necessary to teach your child of taking responsibilities of family. This would make them more responsible and family oriented person. Firstly explain the importance of family, each other's support, respect for parents, and elders, supporting and protecting siblings, family traditions, ancestors, understanding priority of each member, likes and dislikes of each member, staying together as a team family more than money. Then motivate and encourage them to take up responsibilities of family members. Guide them and see how they are fulfilling your wish. If each child is taught importance of family and relationships than no separation would occur in families. All would stay as an ideal family. In a family if one member gains success, then whole family is succeeded. Similarly if one member fails then whole family fails. Just like in sports if one player makes the goal or run, then whole team is considered for it.

Teaching values and ethics- till now how you have given good values and ethics to your child. But now in this age just remind them to lead a ideal life. By this they won't go to wrong route on whatever situation life gives. Teach them and make a habit of reminding values and ethics daily along with challenges. See whether they are following values even during challenges or they are compromising it. The more values are reminded there are lesser chances of them getting to wrong route.

According to me, "be best version of yourself to have best things in life". At least by end of their professional course or education your child should be ready to face the world and take up responsibilities with family values and ethics. That's the real and final success of your parenting journey. And now start your retirement life. I hope you have enjoyed the trailer in this stage, now enjoy the movie in next part. Happy parenting!!!

PART 5

PARENTING DURING LAST STAGE

When Your Child Has His/her Own Family

#Your Final Role-Enjoying Retirement Life.

Now, you have completed the training and entered the retirement phase. But now your child is ready to start the journey which you have completed just now. Every parent's biggest dream is to have a blessed family for their child. But let me clear it, your role won't finish here, there are lot of things to be done. You are in your retirement phase it doesn't mean you don't have power or control over the family. Till you are there, no one is bigger than you. Even if your children have their family, remember your children are your children, their family is also your family. You have equal rights on them also.

When your child gets married, you get a new child in form of son-in-law or daughter-in-law. As we say husband and wife are soul mates or equal partners similarly for parents both should be equal. Both should be considered as one. You have to give equal place as of your child in your heart and life. Then only your children and their family would be yours or else there will be a gap between each other. Just as you and your in-laws, your parents and your life partner.

I agree it will take time to bond with all, as he/she would be a new member. In order to make equal place in your life efforts are needed from both sides. You may think who should say those things to my daughter-in-law or son-in-law, don't say anything just do by actions. As actions speak louder than words. Teach your child to bond with his/her in laws and make equal place in family and their lives. By seeing your efforts, your child's in laws would make similar efforts, your child's in laws would make similar effect on their child towards you. Then see how beautiful would it be if both families merge mutually that is real definition of marriage.

According to me, marriage is not just union of two people but union of two families, two different ideologies and traditions. It is not about finding a right partner but being a right partner. Whatever

you are you get that. So try to be bestest version of yourself, you will get best life partner, deserve best children and best life. Thus teach your child about being right partner for ideal married life.

Bonding with your Daughter-in-Law or your Daughter Bonding with her In-Laws

As I said when your child gets married you get a second child, and forming a mother-daughter relationship immediately is not possible, as she is not your biological child, forming a strong bond with her takes lot of time and patience. **According to me, "I think it's better to adjust for initial years until you three form a bond than struggling for whole life". As this situation is new for both of you, but being elder you should step first.**

Acceptance- firstly in an relationship complete acceptance is required. Until your convinced don't go for marriage. But not always you would get ideal daughter-in-law who will fit according to your mould. You have to change her according to your family needs. For that accept her as she is and then slowly teach her your family values as your daughter. Similarly applies to your daughter to accept her in-laws as they are and put efforts to accept their values and traditions and implement it.

Positive attitude- as parent, you see only good things in your child even in their mistakes, and then guide them how to rectify it. But your intension would only be to see them as perfect. Similarly it applies to your daughter-in-law. If you train your brain to see only good and that all you will see. You can guide her to rectify her mistakes as you guide your child. And you can see by this behaviour the bond would be more stronger and also things would be easy. Similarly it applies to your daughter to have a positive attitude towards her in laws, she should always respect and care them, even if they scold. You can't expect someone to be perfect until you be.

Avoid wrong attitude- your child loves this women, no matter that you can't understand what he can see in her. No matter what your true feelings are, never say negative words against her to your child. There is lot of difference between opinions and bad mouthing. Try to avoid being rude or negative and instead offer up ways you can reconnect. By seeing your behaviour even your daughter-in-law would also do same for you. With this back speaking it would create gap between all of you. Similarly applies to your daughter to not to step between mother and son. She should remember that, she is creator of her husband. She should value and respect that. To save a relation any one has to compromise their ego.

There is no competition- each member has their own role and value in a family. So there is no need to feel insecure. This is what happens between mother-in-law and daughter-in-law relationships. Controlling and then invading each other's space to lessen the threat they feel from each other. Why there is a need for competition. Both of you play equal role in your child's life. Of course one has given the life and other has given the purpose of life. If you want your son or husband to lead a happy and successful life, both of you should be in one team.

Healthy communication- the key for healthy relationship is a result of healthy communication. Sometimes it is important to keep openness in one's approach to let the person in. Your daughter-in-law may have different views and ideologies, explore that and give her chance to apply it. She is also a part of family. Even its important for your daughter to accept her mother-in-law's ideologies and implement it. As she is most important and elder person of the family. She should respect that. All such communications can be communicated as long as the channel is kept open so it is important for both to at least have a cup of coffee or tea daily and discuss each other's concerns, work and how each of wish to work on them. Respect and accept each other's views. Expecting the other to do everything is where the problem arises. Work on it as team work not as individual responsibility.

Bonding with your Son-in-Law or Son with his In-Laws

Even your son-in-law is a part of your family. Not only accept him for your daughter but treat him as your son.

Acceptance- As a parent, it's your responsibility to find an ideal partner for your daughter and embrace him and his family as they are. Welcome your son-in-law into your family with open arms, treating him as your own son, not with fear for your daughter's future. Similarly, teach your son to respect his in-laws and accept them as his own family. Building mutual respect and unity strengthens relationships and creates a harmonious bond between families.

Leave your daughter or daughter-in-law in charge of trying to change your son-in-law or son- If you notice any shortcomings in your son-in-law or son, trust your daughter or daughter-in-law to handle the situation. Offer guidance and support when needed, but avoid directly interfering in their married life. This approach allows them to grow and manage their responsibilities while maintaining harmony in the family.

Responsibilities- Have faith in your son and son-in-law, that he will care for and protect his wife. Be patient and avoid interfering in their married life unless absolutely necessary. This approach allows your son and son-in-law to fulfill their responsibilities. Share your experiences in managing family matters to guide them effectively, as wisdom from a father and father-in-law can help them navigate their roles better.

Spend time together- The bond between a father and son, as well as between a father-in-law and son-in-law, is crucial for a harmonious family. Spending quality time together fosters understanding and creates a positive atmosphere. A woman thrives when supported by the two key men in her life—her father and her husband. By working as a team, you can ensure her happiness and success while strengthening the connection between generations.

Your Final Role!!!

Now that you have formed a strong and meaningful bond with your new family members—your son-in-law or daughter-in-law—you can look forward to enjoying your retirement alongside your loved ones. Soon, your investment in nurturing relationships will take on a new form with the arrival of grandchildren.

Share your parenting experiences with your children so they, too, can embrace and cherish this beautiful and precious journey of parenthood.

As we reach the conclusion of this book, it's important to remember that the journey of learning and growth continues as long as life does. I apologize for any mistakes or omissions in my writing. While I may not have reached perfection, I have made every effort to learn from observations, refer to experts, and present my thoughts sincerely.

No single work can fully capture the beauty of this journey. It is crucial to acknowledge that every child is unique, every parent is unique, and therefore, every parenting experience is distinct.

I hope this book serves as a helpful reference or source of support in your parenting journey. Lastly, I would like to say that parenthood is not just a journey but a profound feeling that elevates a person to a divine status.

Thank you, and Happy Parenting!